# REGENTS ENGLISH WORKBOOK

## GRAMMAR—COMMON USAGE —IDIOMS—VOCABULARY

**Book I**
**Elementary — Intermediate**

### ROBERT J. DIXSON

**REGENTS PUBLISHING COMPANY, INC.**

# TO THE TEACHER

There is no need here to describe the different types of exercises which this book contains or to discuss their wide variety and extent. A glance through the following pages is enough to acquaint anyone with the book's general contents.

Since this is a workbook, there is also little to say as to how it should be used. Each exercise carries its own instructions, and the students proceed accordingly. On the other hand, there are a few points of general pedagogy which the teacher using the book should keep in mind.

First, this is a workbook, and all explanatory material has been kept at a minimum. Thus, the book is not designed to be used alone, or to replace completely the regular classroom text. Rather, this book should be used to supplement the regular classroom text, to give needed variety to the lesson or to provide additional drill materials on important points of grammar and usage.

Second, as a teacher using this book, don't assume that after a student has written the answers to an exercise correctly he knows the material thoroughly and can use the principle in his everyday speech. The exercise is often only the beginning. Much drill and practice are still necessary. Therefore, ask questions, or introduce simple conversation, involving the particular grammar principle. Also, don't hesitate to repeat the exercises in the book several times. Run over these exercises orally in class. If the students have already written the answers in their books, they can cover these answers with their hand or with a separate sheet of paper. Continue to review past exercises which seem important to you, or which have given the students difficulty.

Third, don't fall into the further error of assuming that some of the exercises in this book are too easy for your particular students. Certain exercises may seem easy to you—especially if you speak English as a native—but they still represent a real challenge to anyone studying English as a foreign language. In this connection there is one additional point of utmost importance which should be kept in mind. We are not interested in these exercises in tricking or even in *testing* the student. The exercises are not designed to find out how much a student knows or does not know. Their purpose is simply to drill the student on certain basic points of grammar and usage. The exercises are practice exercises—nothing more. They provide just another means of having students repeat materials which can be learned only through continuous use. For this reason, the exercises have been made as simple and clear as possible. For the same reason a good deal of direct repetition has been purposely introduced, not only in individual exercises but throughout the book.

There are two workbooks in the series, Book I and Book II. Book I is for the elementary and low intermediate student. Book II is for the high intermediate and advanced student. As regards the exact division of materials between the two books, this plan was followed: The exercises in Book I more or less parallel the development by lessons of the materials in *Beginning Lesson In English* published by the Regents Publishing Company. Similarly, Book II follows the general development of the lessons in *Second Book in English,* also published by the Regents Publishing Company.

This does not mean, however, that the workbooks must be used only in conjunction with these two particular books. On the contrary, they are readily adaptable to many uses and can serve effectively to supplement any standard classroom textbook. An answer book, covering all the exercises in each of the books, is available to teachers upon request.

R.J.D.

Miami, Florida
April, 1956.

# TABLE OF CONTENTS

**VERB *To Be*:** The verb *to be* has these forms in the present tense

| I am | we are |
|------|--------|
| you are | you are |
| he, she, it is | they are |

In the blanks at the right, insert the correct form of the verb *to be:*

1.  I ............ a student.       __(am)__

2.  Henry ............ a student.

3.  This ............ a good book.

4.  John and Mary ............ good students.

5.  We ............ also good students.

6.  Mr. Smith ............ a teacher.

7.  He ............ a good teacher.

8.  Miss Smith ............ a woman.

9.  Mr. Jones ............ a man.

10.  You ............ a good student.

11.  Helen and Mary ............ good students.

12.  They ............ sisters.

13.  The windows ............ open.

14.  The door ............ closed.

15.  Today ............ Monday.

16.  This ............ a good exercise.

17.  William and Henry ............ good students.

18.  They ............ brothers.

19.  I ............ very busy today.

20.  Henry ............ also busy today.

21.  We ............ busy.

22.  You and Henry ............ brothers.

23.  I ............ tired now.

## VERB *To Be* (continued)

Choose the correct form and write in the blanks at right.

1. John (is, are) a good student.      ___(is)___

2. We (am, are) good students.      _____

3. Today (is, are) Monday.      _____

4. This (is, are) a good exercise.      _____

5. William and George (is, are) brothers.      _____

6. They (is, are) good students.      _____

7. I (am, is) a student of English.      _____

8. The window (is, are) open.      _____

9. Both doors (is, are) closed.      _____

10. John and I (am, are) in the same class.      _____

11. We (am, are) brothers.      _____

12. Miss Smith (is, are) a teacher.      _____

13. She (is, are) a very good teacher.      _____

14. Mr. Jones (is, am) a teacher.      _____

15. He (is, are) also a good teacher.      _____

16. Mr. and Mrs. Reese (is, are) Americans.      _____

17. You (am, are) a good student.      _____

18. I (am, is) also a good student.      _____

19. The weather today (is, are) good.      _____

20. This (is, are) a good exercise.      _____

21. She and Mary (is, are) sisters.      _____

22. You and Henry (is, are) brothers.      _____

2

**VERB *To Be*; NEGATIVE FORM:** We form the negative of the verb *to be* by putting *not* after the verb.

> I am *not* a teacher.
> Henry is *not* a good student.

---

Change to negative. In the blanks at the right, write the verb of each sentence followed by *not*.

1. We are brothers.      (are not) _____

2. Today is Monday. _____

3. She and Mary are sisters. _____

4. I am a good student. _____

5. This is a difficult exercise. _____

6. Miss Jones is a good teacher. _____

7. Mr. and Mrs. Jones are Americans. _____

8. She is a good friend. _____

9. They are busy today. _____

10. You and Henry are cousins. _____

11. John and I are in the same class. _____

12. William is busy today. _____

13. We are busy today. _____

14. Henry and he are first cousins. _____

15. You are a good student. _____

16. You and George are good friends. _____

17. Mary and I are good friends. _____

18. The door is closed. _____

19. Both windows are open. _____

20. They are brothers. _____

21. We are friends. _____

22. They are new students. _____

3

**VERB *To Be*; QUESTION FORM:** We form questions with the verb *to be* by placing the verb before the subject.

*Are* you a teacher or a student?
*Is* John a good student?

Change to questions. In the blanks at the right, insert the verb of each sentence followed by the subject.

1. They are cousins. (Are they) _____

2. He is a bad student. _____

3. Today is Tuesday. _____

4. John and he are in the same class. _____

5. You and George are cousins. _____

6. She and Mary are good friends. _____

7. Both windows are closed. _____

8. The door is wide open. _____

9. They are new students. _____

10. Henry and she are first cousins. _____

11. We are busy today. _____

12. Mr. and Mrs. Jones are Americans. _____

13. This is a difficult exercise. _____

14. This lesson is easy. _____

15. She is a good teacher. _____

16. Helen and she are sisters. _____

17. You and Henry are in the same class. _____

18. I am tired today. _____

19. The teacher is tired. _____

20. This is a good book. _____

21. They are old friends. _____

22. He is a tall man. _____

**VERB *To Have*:** The verb *to have* has these forms in the present tense.

| | |
|---|---|
| I have | we have |
| you have | you have |
| he, she, it has | they have |

---

In the blanks at the right, insert the correct form of the verb *to have:*

1. Helen ............ a new hat. (has)<br>--------

2. I ............ many friends in this class. ........

3. We ............ new English books. ........

4. You ............ a good fountain-pen. ........

5. The dog ............ a long tail. ........

6. This book ................ a red cover. ........

7. I ............ a new copybook. ........

8. Mary ............ a new dress. ........

9. John ............ a new watch. ........

10. John and Henry ............ many friends. ........

11. We ............ pencils but no pens. ........

12. I ............ two sisters but no brothers. ........

13. John ............ two brothers but no sisters. ........

14. Miss Smith ............ a new typewriter. ........

15. The teacher ............ red hair. ........

16. You ............ brown eyes. ........

17. I ............ blue eyes. ........

18. The cat ............ green eyes. ........

19. We all ............ new copybooks. ........

20. George and I ............ new fountain-pens. ........

21. This room ............ many windows. ........

22. The teacher ............ a bad cold today. ........

5

**VERB *To Have*:** NEGATIVE FORM: We form the negative of *to have* by placing *not* after the verb.* In everyday conversation we generally use the contractions *haven't* or *hasn't*.

> I *haven't* (have not) a new book.
> John *hasn't* (has not) a pencil.

---

Change to negative form. In the blanks at the right, fill in the verb of each sentence, followed by *not*. Use contracted forms only.

1. She has a new hat.                 (hasn't) _____

2. They have many friends in the United States. _____

3. Helen has red hair. _____

4. The cat has green eyes. _____

5. That room has many windows. _____

6. Mary has a bad cold. _____

7. I have two sisters. _____

8. John has two brothers. _____

9. This book has a red cover. _____

10. We have two different English books. _____

11. He has a new automobile. _____

12. The men have their coats *on*. _____

13. John has his coat *off*. _____

14. Helen has blue eyes. _____

15. I have a dog. _____

16. Mary has a cat. _____

17. The cat has a short tail. _____

18. The dog has a long nose. _____

19. I have a good fountain-pen. _____

20. John and Henry have many friends in this class. _____

* We may also use the auxiliaries *do* and *does* to form the negative of *to have*. See later exercises.

**VERB *To Have*; QUESTION FORM:** We form questions with the verb *to have* by placing the verb before the subject.*

Have you a new fountain pen?
Has Helen a new hat?

---

Change to questions. In the blanks at the right, fill in the verb of each sentence, followed by the subject.

1. She has a new hat.                                    (Has she) _____

2. This room has three doors.                            _____

3. That girl has very long hair.                         _____

4. You have a dog.                                       _____

5. Helen has many friends in this class.                 _____

6. The cat has a long tail.                              _____

7. Both these dogs have long noses.                      _____

8. Mary has red hair.                                    _____

9. You have a bad cold today.                            _____

10. Mr. Smith has his coat off.                          _____

11. John has his hat on.                                 _____

12. We have different English books.                     _____

13. This book has a blue cover.                          _____

14. Mr. Smith has a new automobile.                      _____

15. You have a new watch.                                _____

16. Every watch has two hands and a face.                _____

17. Every student in the class has a copybook.           _____

18. We all have new fountain-pens.                       _____

19. Helen has a bad headache.                            _____

20. Miss Smith has a new typewriter.                     _____

* We may also use the auxiliaries *do* and *does* to form questions with the verb *to have*. See later exercises.

7

**SIMPLE PRESENT TENSE:** The simple present tense of all verbs in English (except the verb *to be*) has the same form as the infinitive. In the third person singular, however, *s* is added. We use this tense to describe an action which goes on every day or in general.

| | |
|---|---|
| I work | we work |
| you work | you work |
| he, she, it works | they work |

---

Write the correct form of the verb in parentheses, in the blanks at the right.

1. John (speak) English well. _(speaks)_

2. We (write) many letters. _____

3. I (walk) to school with John every day. _____

4. Henry (walk) to school with Mary. _____

5. I always (sit) in this seat. _____

6. Henry always (sit) in that seat. _____

7. The students (write) many exercises every day. _____

8. John always (open) the windows for the teacher. _____

9. Mr. Smith (work) in this room. _____

10. He (smoke) many cigarettes. _____

11. I (come) to school by bus. _____

12. Henry also (come) to school by bus. _____

13. George and his brother (walk) to school. _____

14. I (read) the newspaper every day. _____

15. We (eat) in the cafeteria every day. _____

16. Mr. Smith also (eat) in the cafeteria every day. _____

17. I (play) tennis every afternoon. _____

18. John also (play) tennis every afternoon. _____

19. Many students (play) tennis every afternoon. _____

20. Helen (work) very hard. _____

21. She (want) to learn English. _____

8

## PRESENT TENSE (continued)

Verbs ending in the letter *y*, preceded by a consonant, change this *y* to *i* and then add *es* in the third person singular of the present tense (Examples: study, studies; marry, marries). Verbs ending in *o* generally add *es* in the third person singular (Examples: go, goes; do, does). Verbs ending in an *s* sound *(s, sh, ch, x,* or *z)* also add *es* in the third person singular (Examples: wish, wishes; pass, passes).

---

Choose the correct form and then write this form in the blanks at the right:

1. I (study, studies) English every day.  (study) _____

2. John also (study, studies) English every day.  _____

3. Helen (go, goes) to the movies very often.  _____

4. I seldom (go, goes) to the movies.  _____

5. William (carry, carries) his books in a briefcase.  _____

6. The teacher also (carry, carries) his books in a briefcase.  _____

7. Frank (play, plays) the violin very well.  _____

8. Mary (play, plays) the piano very well.  _____

9. We (play, plays) tennis every afternoon.  _____

10. George and Henry also (play, plays) tennis every afternoon.  _____

11. George (does, do) this exercise very well.  _____

12. Helen also (do, does) this exercise very well.  _____

13. I always (try, tries) to come to school on time.  _____

14. You always (try, tries) to come to school on time.  _____

15. William also (try, tries) to come to school on time.  _____

16. I (wish, wishes) to learn English.  _____

17. John also (wish, wishes) to learn English.  _____

18. Mr. and Mrs. Smith (go, goes) to the movies very often.  _____

19. Mr. Smith (teach, teaches) English and French.  _____

20. The nurse (watch, watches) the child in the park.  _____

21. Mr. and Mrs. Jones both (teach, teaches) English.  _____

22. Mrs. Jones also (teach, teaches) mathematics.  _____

9

## PRESENT TENSE (continued); *He* and *I*

Change each of the sentences below so that it begins with *he* instead of *I*. Write *he* followed by the correct form of the verb in the blanks at the right.

1. I study English every day.      (He studies) ----------

2. I like to study English.      ----------

3. I live in Miami.      ----------

4. I am a good student.      ----------

5. I wish to learn English well.      ----------

6. I teach English.      ----------

7. I am very busy today.      ----------

8. I go to the movies very often.      ----------

9. I do these exercises every day.      ----------

10. I see Mr. Smith on the bus every day.      ----------

11. I am a careful student.      ----------

12. I carry my books to school in a briefcase.      ----------

13. I have English lessons every day.      ----------

14. I study English with Mr. Smith.      ----------

15. I play tennis very often.      ----------

16. I always try to come to school on time.      ----------

17. I eat lunch in the cafeteria every day.      ----------

18. I try to speak English well.      ----------

19. I study very hard.      ----------

20. I pass Mr. Smith on the street every day.      ----------

21. I always go to school with John.      ----------

22. I have two brothers.      ----------

(NOTE: Repeat the above exercise, changing *I* to *John*. Repeat, changing *I* to *we*, etc.)

10

**PLURAL FORM:** (a) Most nouns in English form their plural by adding *s* to the singular (Examples: book, books; door, doors, etc.) (b) Nouns, however, which end in an *s* sound *(s, sh, ch, x* or *z)* add *es* to form the plural (Examples: church, churches; box, boxes; kiss, kisses, etc.) (c) A few nouns have special forms in the plural (Examples: man, men; woman, women; child, children; foot, feet; tooth, teeth; mouse, mice).

---

In the blanks at the right of each word, write the plural form:

| | | | |
|---|---|---|---|
| 1. book | (books) | 23. box | (boxes) |
| 2. student | _____ | 24. sister | _____ |
| 3. class | _____ | 25. hat | _____ |
| 4. brother | _____ | 26. man | _____ |
| 5. friend | _____ | 27. coat | _____ |
| 6. cousin | _____ | 28. tooth | _____ |
| 7. watch | _____ | 29. cover | _____ |
| 8. cafeteria | _____ | 30. automobile | _____ |
| 9. door | _____ | 31. child | _____ |
| 10. window | _____ | 32. dog | _____ |
| 11. wish | _____ | 33. foot | _____ |
| 12. teacher | _____ | 34. cat | _____ |
| 13. pencil | _____ | 35. hand | _____ |
| 14. pen | _____ | 36. church | _____ |
| 15. copybook | _____ | 37. face | _____ |
| 16. match | _____ | 38. headache | _____ |
| 17. tail | _____ | 39. dish | _____ |
| 18. eye | _____ | 40. cigarette | _____ |
| 19. nose | _____ | 41. school | _____ |
| 20. dress | _____ | 42. bus | _____ |
| 21. woman | _____ | 43. mouse | _____ |
| 22. lunch | _____ | 44. kiss | _____ |

## PLURAL FORM (continued)

Change the italicized word from singular to plural. Then also make the necessary change in the form of the verb.

1. The *book* is on the desk.                          (The books are) _____

2. The *man* speaks English well.                      _____

3. The *boy* plays in the park.                         _____

4. The *child* plays with the dog.                      _____

5. The *mouse* runs into the hole.                      _____

6. The *cat* runs after the mouse.                      _____

7. *He* speaks English well.                            _____

8. *I* play tennis every afternoon.                     _____

9. *She* goes to school on the bus.                     _____

10. The *bus* always arrives on time.                   _____

11. The *class* begins at one o'clock.                  _____

12. The *woman* is in the store.                        _____

13. The *dish* is on the table.                         _____

14. The *woman* is busy.                                _____

15. The *man* is also busy.                             _____

16. The *dress* is pretty.                              _____

17. The *pencil* is on the desk.                        _____

18. The *train* leaves at eight o'clock.                _____

19. The *watch* runs well.                              _____

20. The *box* is yellow.                                _____

21. The *church* is very large.                         _____

22. The *class* ends at two o'clock.                    _____

23. The *bus* is full.                                  _____

24. The *child* is sick.                                _____

12

## POSSESSIVE ADJECTIVES: The personal pronouns in English with their corresponding possessive adjectives follow:

| | |
|---|---|
| I — my | we — our |
| you — your | you — your |
| she — her | they — their |
| he — his | |
| it — its | |

---

Write the *possessive adjective* which corresponds with the subject of the sentence in the blanks at the right.

1. The boy walks to ............ chair.                                    (his)
   _____

2. The girl walks to ............ chair.                                   _____

3. I walk to ............ chair.                                           _____

4. We study ............ lessons every night.                             _____

5. I put ............ copybook on the desk.                               _____

6. Mary likes ............ English class.                                 _____

7. We bring ............ copybooks to the lesson.                         _____

8. The boys bring ............ copybooks to the lesson.                   _____

9. The girls bring ............ copybooks to the lesson.                  _____

10. Our teacher, Mr. Smith, comes to school in ............ car.          _____

11. John studies English in ............ room.                            _____

12. I study in ............ room.                                         _____

13. The dog chases ............ tail.                                     _____

14. The cat eats ............ dinner.                                     _____

15. I often look at ............ watch during the lesson.                 _____

16. Miss Jones, our teacher, often looks at ............ watch
    during the lesson.                                                    _____

17. Many of the students look at ............ watches during
    the lesson.                                                          _____

18. You write many words in ............ copybook every day.              _____

19. Grace always writes many words in ............ copybook.              _____

20. I never write the new words in ............ copybook.                 _____

21. The children play with ............ toys.                             _____

22. We always prepare ............ homework every day.                    _____

13

**THERE IS; THERE ARE:** *There is* and *there are* are important phrases in English; they correspond to the Spanish and Portuguese *hay* and the French *il y a*. We use *there is* with singular nouns; we use *there are* with plural nouns (Examples: *There is* a book on the table. *There are* two magazines on the desk.).

---

Write the correct form in the blanks at the right:

1. There (is, are) a magazine on the chair.  (is) _____
2. There (is, are) two men in the office.  _____
3. There (is, are) many children in the park.  _____
4. There (is, are) many people on the bus.  _____
5. There (is, are) a man at the door.  _____
6. There (is, are) seven days in a week.  _____
7. There (is, are) twelve months in a year.  _____
8. There (is, are) a rug on the floor.  _____
9. There (is, are) two windows in this room.  _____
10. There (is, are) many students in our class.  _____
11. There (is, are) many English classes in our school.  _____
12. There (is, are) only one chair in this room.  _____
13. There (is, are) several pictures on the wall.  _____
14. There (is, are) only one cloud in the sky.  _____
15. There (is, are) two dishes on the table.  _____
16. There (is, are) many churches in this city.  _____
17. There (is, are) two women in Mr. Smith's office.  _____
18. There (is, are) nobody in the room.  _____
19. There (is, are) someone at the door.  _____
20. There (is, are) many new words in this lesson.  _____
21. There (is, are) a new student in our class.  _____
22. There (is, are) a letter here for you.  _____

14

**THERE IS; THERE ARE;** NEGATIVE FORM: The negative form of *there is* and *there are* is obtained regularly by placing *not* after the verb (Examples: There *is not* one cloud in the sky. There *are not* many students in our class). In everyday conversation, however, the contractions *isn't* and *aren't* are generally used (Examples: There *isn't* one cloud in the sky. There *aren't* many students in our class.).

---

Change to negative form. Write the verb of each sentence, followed by *not*. Use contracted forms only.

1. There are many chairs in this room. _(aren't)_

2. There is a radio in each room. _____

3. There is a policeman on the corner. _____

4. There are many offices in that building. _____

5. There are many new students in our class. _____

6. There are many children in the park. _____

7. There is a typewriter in each room. _____

8. There are many magazines on the desk. _____

9. There is a window in the room. _____

10. There are two doors in the room. _____

11. There are many churches in this city. _____

12. There is a rug on the floor. _____

13. There are two men in the office. _____

14. There is a letter here for you. _____

15. There are many clouds in the sky. _____

16. There are many new words in this lesson. _____

17. There is a mouse in this room. _____

18. There is one girl in our class. _____

19. There are many exercises in this lesson. _____

20. There is a library in this building. _____

21. There are two telephones in the office. _____

22. There is a blackboard in our classroom. _____

15

**THERE IS; THERE ARE; QUESTION FORM:** The question form of *there is* and *there are* is obtained regularly by placing the verb before the word *there* (Examples: *Is there* a pencil on the desk? *Are there* many students in your class? How many days *are there* in a week?)

---

Change to questions. In the blanks at the right, write the verb of each sentence followed by *there*.

1. There is a policeman on the corner. _(Is there)_____

2. There are many students in our class. _____

3. There is a typewriter in each class. _____

4. There is a window in each room. _____

5. There is a letter here for you. _____

6. There are many clouds in the sky today. _____

7. There are several new words in this lesson. _____

8. There is a library in this building. _____

9. There is no blackboard in our classroom. _____

10. There are two telephones in the office. _____

11. There is a mouse in the room. _____

12. There are many churches in this city. _____

13. There is a rug on the floor. _____

14. There are many birds in the tree. _____

15. There are several magazines on the table. _____

16. There is a radio in every room. _____

17. There is only one chair in the room. _____

18. There are only two dishes on the table. _____

19. There are many English classes in our school. _____

20. There are twelve months in a year. _____

21. There are only a few people on the bus. _____

22. There are several pictures on the wall. _____

16

**THE INDEFINITE ARTICLE:** The Indefinite article *a* is changed to *an* before any word beginning with a vowel (a, e, i, o, u) or with a vowel sound. Examples: *a* book, *an* apple, *an* old man, *an* (h)our.

In the blanks, write the correct indefinite article, *a* or *an*:

1. ___(a)___ Frenchman
2. ___(an)___ Englishman
3. _____ German
4. _____ book
5. _____ apple
6. _____ student
7. _____ umbrella
8. _____ banana
9. _____ orange
10. _____ horse
11. _____ elephant
12. _____ egg
13. _____ argument
14. _____ month
15. _____ hour
16. _____ article
17. _____ friend
18. _____ idea
19. _____ house
20. _____ car
21. _____ automobile
22. _____ lsland

23. _____ easy exercise
24. _____ difficult exercise
25. _____ honest man
26. _____ big house
27. _____ old house
28. _____ important lesson
29. _____ unimportant lesson
30. _____ good lesson
31. _____ bad lesson
32. _____ interesting lesson
33. _____ uninteresting lesson
34. _____ easy lesson
35. _____ very easy lesson
36. _____ late class
37. _____ early class
38. _____ very early class
39. _____ excellent teacher
40. _____ cheap car
41. _____ expensive car
42. _____ nice girl
43. _____ English book
44. _____ French book

17

**THIS, THAT, THESE, THOSE:** We use *this* to refer to something near us; we use *that* to refer to something at a distance (Examples: *This* book in my hand is new. *That* pencil over there on the table belongs to the teacher.). The plural form of *this* is *these;* the plural form of *that* is *those.*

---

Change the italicized word or words to plural form and write them in the blanks. Also include corresponding change in verb.

1. *This book* is new.      (These books are)

2. *That car* belongs to Mr. Jones.   ( Those cars belong)

3. *That man* in the office is my friend.   --------------

4. *This apple* is very good.   --------------

5. *This exercise* is very difficult.   --------------

6. *That pocketbook* on the table belongs to Mary.   --------------

7. *This lesson* is very interesting.   --------------

8. *This** is an interesting lesson.   --------------

9. *That automobile* belongs to my father.   --------------

10. *That** is my father's automobile.   --------------

11. *That window* over there is open.   --------------

12. *That* is the office of the president.   --------------

13. *This letter* is for you.   --------------

14. *That letter* is for Mr. Smith.   --------------

15. *That house* near the corner is very old.   --------------

16. *This umbrella* belongs to Mary.   --------------

17. *This exercise* is very easy for me.   --------------

18. *This* is an easy exercise for me.   --------------

19. *That* is my hat.   --------------

20. *That hat* belongs to me.   --------------

21. *That cloud* in the sky looks very dark.   --------------

22. *This English class* is always interesting.   --------------

* Notice that in English *this* and *that* are used both as pronouns and as adjectives without any change in form.

**REVIEW:** Choose the correct form and write it in the blanks.

1. Henry (is, are) a good student.                               ___(is)___

2. (This, These) books belong to Helen.                          _____

3. Henry and she (is, are) first cousins.                        _____

4. He (have, has) many friends in our class.                     _____

5. I (haven't, hasn't) a good fountain-pen.                      _____

6. John (speak, speaks) English well.                            _____

7. I (come, comes) to school by bus.                             _____

8. There are two (church, churches) on this street.              _____

9. In autumn the (leafs, leaves) fall from the trees.            _____

10. (Tomatos, Tomatoes) are my favorite vegetable.               _____

11. (Have, has) Helen a new hat?                                 _____

12. The dog chases (its, it's) tail.                             _____

13. There (is, are) seven days in a week.                        _____

14. There (isn't, aren't) a window in the room.                  _____

15. This is (a, an) English book.                                _____

16. Mr. Smith is (a, an) old man.                                _____

17. I spend (a, an) hour on my homework every day.               _____

18. (That, Those) magazines belong to Helen.                     _____

19. Mr. Smith (teach, teaches) English and French.               _____

20. John always (try, tries) to come to school on time.          _____

21. You and George (is, are) good friends.                       _____

22. Grace and Helen (has, have) many friends in this school.     _____

23. There (is, are) nobody in the office.                        _____

24. This is (a, an) difficult exercise.                          _____

25. He is (a, an) honest man.                                    _____

19

**IMPERATIVE FORM:** To obtain the imperative in English, which is the form used to express a command or strong request, we use the infinitive without *to*. There is only one form for both singular and plural, and the subject *you* is understood but not expressed (Examples: *Wait here. Come back later.*) The negative of the imperative is formed with *do not*, which is usually contracted in everyday speech to *don't* (Examples: *Don't wait here. Don't come back later.*)

---

Change these imperative sentences to negative form. Use the contraction *don't*. Write *don't*, followed by the verb of each sentence, in the blank spaces.

1. Write your exercises in pencil.                          (Don't write) _____

2. Come back at two o'clock.                                _____

3. Sit in that chair.                                       _____

4. Open the window.                                         _____

5. Close the door.                                          _____

6. Ask Mr. Smith to come in.                                _____

7. Take the next bus.                                       _____

8. Wait on that corner.                                     _____

9. Put your books there on that chair.                      _____

10. Hang your coat on that chair.                           _____

11. Study the next lesson.                                  _____

12. Write all the exercises in this lesson.                 _____

13. Help John with his lesson.                              _____

14. Speak Spanish in the lesson.                            _____

15. Use the new words in this lesson.                       _____

16. Give this to Mr. Smith.                                 _____

17. Sit in the sun.                                         _____

18. Drive fast.                                             _____

19. Tell Mary to wait for us.                               _____

20. Look out the window.                                    _____

21. Put these chairs in the next room.                      _____

22. Look up all the new words in your dictionary.           _____

**PERSONAL PRONOUNS; OBJECTIVE CASE:** The objective case forms of the personal pronouns follow:

| Nominative | Objective | Nominative | Objective |
|---|---|---|---|
| I | me | we | us |
| you | you | you | you |
| he | him | they | them |
| she | her | | |
| it | it | | |

Note: The objective case forms are used as direct or indirect objects of the verb, as objects of all prepositions, etc.

---

Choose the correct form and write it in the blanks at the right.

1. I see (he, him) on the bus every day.  (him)

2. He sits near (I, me) at the lesson.

3. I go with (she, her) to the movies very often.

4. We often see (they, them) at school.

5. I like (she, her) very much.

6. I know both (he, him) and his brother very well.

7. He sits near (we, us) at the lesson.

8. Don't speak to (they, them) in Spanish.

9. I often go with (they, them) to the movies.

10. He often helps (I, me) with my lessons.

11. She writes many letters to (he, him).

12. Don't lend money to (she, her).

13. Mr. Jones teaches (we, us) English.

14. He gives many presents to (she, her).

15. Please explain this exercise to (me, I).

16. Please give this book to (him, he).

17. Don't go with (them, they) to the movie tonight.

18. The teacher always explains the lesson to (we, us).

19. He wants to talk with (me, I).

20. I like (they, them) very much.

21. He seldom speaks to (us, we).

21

# PERSONAL PRONOUNS; OBJECTIVE CASE (continued)

For the italicized word or words in each sentence, substitute the correct objective case personal pronoun.

1. I see *John* on the bus every morning. _____(him)_____

2. I often go to the movies with *Mary*. _____

3. I like *John and Henry* very much. _____

4. He never speaks to *Mary and me*. _____

5. I also like *Mary and Helen* very much. _____

6. She writes many letters to *her sister*. _____

7. I sit near *William and his brother*. _____

8. I see *Helen* in the cafeteria every day. _____

9. I understand *my teacher, Mr. Jones*, very well. _____

10. He gives *his son* much money. _____

11. She always speaks to *her daughter* in Spanish. _____

12. He sends *his sister* many presents. _____

13. John writes many letters to *his aunt*. _____

14. I write many letters to *my uncle*. _____

15. I sit near *Mary and Helen* at the lesson. _____

16. Helen sits near *Henry and George*. _____

17. She says that she sees *you and Henry* on the bus every morning. _____

18. I often see *those boys* in the cafeteria. _____

19. I know both *Henry and his brother* very well. _____

20. I often go to the movies with *my parents*. _____

21. All the girls like *their teacher, Miss Smith*, very well. _____

22. He wants to go with *Henry and me* to the movies tonight. _____

**VOCABULARY REVIEW:** (a) The days of the week are *Monday, Tuesday, Wednesday, Thursday, Friday, Saturday,* and *Sunday.* (b) The months of the year are *January, February, March, April, May, June, July, August, September, October, November,* and *December.* (c) The four seasons of the year are *spring, summer, autumn (fall),* and *winter.*

---

Using the blanks, write the correct word necessary to complete the meaning of the sentence:

1. The first month of the year is .............          (January) _____
2. The second month of the year is .............      _____
3. The third month of the year is .............      _____
4. The last month of the year is .............      _____
5. The month of June comes before the month of .............      _____
6. The month of September comes before the month of .............      _____
7. The month of May comes after the month of .............      _____
8. The month of August comes after the month of .............      _____
9. In the United States, elections take place during the month of .............      _____
10. In the United States, the weather during the months of July and August is generally very .............      _____
11. In the United States, the weather during the months of January and February is generally .............      _____
12. The first day of the week is .............      _____
13. The second day of the week is .............      _____
14. The last day of the week is .............      _____
15. Monday comes before .............      _____
16. Thursday comes before .............      _____
17. Wednesday comes after .............      _____
18. Saturday comes after .............      _____
19. The four seasons of the year are spring, summer, autumn, and .............      _____
20. In the United States, Washington's birthday occurs during the month of .............      _____
21. In the United States, Christmas occurs in the month of .............      _____
22. In the United States, Easter is celebrated during the ............. season.      _____

**VERB *To Be*; PAST TENSE:** The past tense forms of the verb *to be* are as follows:

| | |
|---|---|
| I was | we were |
| you were | you were |
| he, she, it was | they were |

---

Change the verb to past time and write it in the blanks at the right:

1. He *is* a good student. (was)

2. I *am* also a good student. _____

3. John *is* in my class. _____

4. We *are* good friends. _____

5. Helen and Mary *are* in the same class. _____

6. The door *is* open. _____

7. The windows and doors *are* open. _____

8. The book *is* on the table. _____

9. I *am* very hungry. _____

10. Mary and John *are* students. _____

11. Miss Jones *is* our teacher. _____

12. This *is* an easy exercise. _____

13. The weather *is* good. _____

14. Both doors *are* closed. _____

15. This lesson *is* easy. _____

16. You and George *are* good friends. _____

17. Helen and I *are* also good friends. _____

18. You *are* a good student. _____

19. There *is* someone at the door. _____

20. There *are* many students in our class. _____

21. There *is* a magazine on this desk. _____

22. We *are* both students. _____

**PAST TENSE OF REGULAR VERBS:** The past tense of most verbs in English is formed by adding *ed* to the simple (infinitive) form. All such verbs which form their past tense in this way are known as *regular verbs.* Example:

| | |
|---|---|
| I worked | we worked |
| you worked | you worked |
| he, she, it worked | they worked |

If the verb already ends in *e*, then only *d* is added (Examples: use, used; notice, noticed)

---

Change the verb of each sentence to past time and write it in the blanks at right:

1. We always *walk* to school.         (walked)

2. He *arrives* at school on time every day. _____

3. Our lesson *ends* at two o'clock. _____

4. He *lives* in Miami. _____

5. They *study** in our class. _____

6. We *finish* our lessons at three o'clock. _____

7. I *like* to study English. _____

8. Helen *answers* all of the teacher's questions. _____

9. We *walk* through the park every morning. _____

10. The dog *follows* the boy everywhere. _____

11. I *need* a new book. _____

12. We always *wait* for her on this corner. _____

13. He *wants* to learn English. _____

14. We *learn* many new words in this class. _____

15. I *use* my new fountain-pen in every class. _____

16. We *listen* to the radio every night. _____

17. My parents *watch* television every night. _____

18. They *expect* to go to Europe in July. _____

19. I *prefer* to study in this class. _____

20. He always *talks* to us in English. _____

* When the simple form of the verb ends in *y*, preceded by a consonant, the *y* is changed to *i* before adding *ed* (Examples: study, *studied*; marry, *married*). Compare with similar change in the third person singular of the present tense (study, *studies*; marry, *marries*, etc.).

25

**PAST TENSE OF REGULAR VERBS; PRONUNCIATION:** When we add *ed* to a verb which ends in the letters *t* or *d*, we pronounce the *ed* as a separate syllable.

count counted (pronounced *count ed*)
wait waited (pronounced *wait ed*)

When, however, we add *ed* to a verb which does not end in *t* or *d*, we do not pronounce the *ed* as a separate syllable.

pull pulled (pronounced *pulled*)
burn burned (pronounced *burned*)

---

Pronounce the following past tense forms. Then in the blank spaces write the numbers 1 or 2 to show whether the word is pronounced as a word of one syllable, or as a word of two syllables.

| | | |
|---|---|---|
| 1. ended ___(2)___ | 21. learned ___(1)___ |
| 2. filled _____ | 22. parted _____ |
| 3. counted _____ | 23. picked _____ |
| 4. rented _____ | 24. looked _____ |
| 5. needed _____ | 25. lived _____ |
| 6. showed _____ | 26. liked _____ |
| 7. planted _____ | 27. lasted _____ |
| 8. worked _____ | 28. closed _____ |
| 9. washed _____ | 29. changed _____ |
| 10. wanted _____ | 30. landed _____ |
| 11. waited _____ | 31. used _____ |
| 12. walked _____ | 32. mailed _____ |
| 13. stopped _____ | 33. handed _____ |
| 14. spelled _____ | 34. crossed _____ |
| 15. smoked _____ | 35. pulled _____ |
| 16. fainted _____ | 36. earned _____ |
| 17. pointed _____ | 37. painted _____ |
| 18. asked _____ | 38. boiled _____ |
| 19. danced _____ | 39. burned _____ |
| 20. talked _____ | 40. touched _____ |

**PAST TENSE OF IRREGULAR VERBS:** Many common verbs in English have special past tense forms. The past tense of these "irregular verbs" must be memorized. Here are a few such verbs with their past tense forms:

| | | |
|---|---|---|
| sit — sat | have — had | put — put |
| write — wrote | eat — ate | come — came |
| read — read | buy — bought | speak — spoke |
| drink — drank | | get — got |

These verbs have the same form in all three persons of the past tense, singular and plural. Example:

| | |
|---|---|
| I sat | we sat |
| you sat | you sat |
| he, she, it sat | they sat |

---

Change to the past time; write the correct form of the verb in the blanks at the right.

1. She writes many letters.                          (wrote) _____

2. He buys many books.                               _____

3. I read the New York Times every morning.          _____

4. She drinks milk with her meals.                   _____

5. He has many friends.                              _____

6. John sits in this seat.                           _____

7. He eats lunch in the cafeteria.                   _____

8. I get up early every morning.                     _____

9. He speaks English well.                           _____

10. He puts his books on this table.                 _____

11. She comes to school by bus.                      _____

12. They have a new car.                             _____

13. She and John always drink coffee for lunch.      _____

14. I always sit near the window.                    _____

15. They speak Spanish.                              _____

16. He gets up at ten o'clock every morning.         _____

17. We eat dinner at home.                           _____

18. He reads many English books.                     _____

19. I buy all my books in the school book-store.     _____

20. We write our exercises in ink.                   _____

27

## VOCABULARY REVIEW; MISTAKES AS TO THE FACTS: In this exercise, correct the mistakes in fact by changing the italicized word or words. Write the correct word in the blanks at the right.

1. The first month of the year is *February*.                    (January)

2. The last month of the year is *November*.                    _____

3. The next to the last month of the year is *October*.         _____

4. September comes *after* October.                             _____

5. July comes *before* June.                                    _____

6. There are *eight* days in a week.                            _____

7. The first day of the week is *Tuesday*.                      _____

8. The last day of the week is *Friday*.                        _____

9. Monday comes *after* Tuesday.                                _____

10. Friday comes *before* Thursday.                             _____

11. The month of February usually has *twenty-nine* days.       _____

12. The four seasons of the year are spring, summer, autumn, and *Christmas*.                                                  _____

13. Spring begins on *June* 21st.                               _____

14. Summer begins on *March* 21st.                              _____

15. The past tense of the irregular verb TO SIT is *set*.       _____

16. The past tense of the verb TO BUY is *buyed*.               _____

17. The plural form of the word CHILD is *childs*.              _____

18. The plural form of the word WOMAN is *womans*.              _____

19. There are *fifty* seconds in a minute.                      _____

20. There are *seventy* minutes in an hour.                     _____

21. The opposite of TALL is *big*.                              _____

22. The opposite of DIFFICULT is *new*.                         _____

28

**VOCABULARY REVIEW - OPPOSITES:** Use the blanks to write in the opposites of the following words.

| | | | | | |
|---|---|---|---|---|---|
| 1. | tall | (short) | 24. | bad | ---------- |
| 2. | open | ---------- | 25. | past | ---------- |
| 3. | in | ---------- | 26. | down | ---------- |
| 4. | good | ---------- | 27. | close | ---------- |
| 5. | yes | ---------- | 28. | out | ---------- |
| 6. | present | ---------- | 29. | no | ---------- |
| 7. | up | ---------- | 30. | down | ---------- |
| 8. | black | ---------- | 31. | absent | ---------- |
| 9. | many | ---------- | 32. | white | ---------- |
| 10. | before | ---------- | 33. | few | ---------- |
| 11. | easy | ---------- | 34. | after | ---------- |
| 12. | push | ---------- | 35. | difficult | ---------- |
| 13. | hot | ---------- | 36. | pull | ---------- |
| 14. | first | ---------- | 37. | cold | ---------- |
| 15. | big | ---------- | 38. | cool | ---------- |
| 16. | cheap | ---------- | 39. | past | ---------- |
| 17. | sweet | ---------- | 40. | last | ---------- |
| 18. | early | ---------- | 41. | little | ---------- |
| 19. | warm | ---------- | 42. | expensive | ---------- |
| 20. | hot | ---------- | 43. | sour | ---------- |
| 21. | day | ---------- | 44. | night | ---------- |
| 22. | sell | ---------- | 45. | stop | ---------- |
| 23. | start | ---------- | 46. | buy | ---------- |

**PREPOSITIONS:** In the blanks at the right, fill in the correct preposition.

1. A man sees ............ his eyes.                           (with)

2. I always eat ............ the cafeteria.                    _____

3. How many months are there ............ a year?             _____

4. January comes ............ February.                        _____

5. April comes ............ March.                             _____

6. Every morning I leave home ............ eight o'clock.      _____

7. I arrive ............ my work at nine o'clock.              _____

8. Sometimes I walk ............ my work.                      _____

9. John put the letter ............ an envelope.               _____

10. Don't sit ............ that chair.                         _____

11. What is the opposite ............ the word *pull?*         _____

12. January is the first month ............ the year.          _____

13. I was late ............ my lesson yesterday.               _____

14. I mailed the letter ............ the mail box.             _____

15. Yesterday John paid my fare ............ the bus.          _____

16. I spoke ............ Mary about that matter.               _____

17. He explained everything ............ me.                   _____

18. I write all the new words ............ my copybook.        _____

19. I get up ............ eight o'clock every morning.         _____

20. They always come to school ............ bus.               _____

21. I like to travel ............ plane.                       _____

22. There is a large blackboard ............ the wall.         _____

23. I had only a sandwich ............ lunch.                  _____

24. Don't write your exercises ............ pencil.            _____

**GENERAL REVIEW:** Choose the correct form and write it in the blanks at the right.

1. William and Mary (is, are) good friends.                    __(are)__

2. Helen (was, were) absent from class yesterday.              _____

3. John (speak, speaks) English well.                          _____

4. Yesterday morning I (get, got) up very late.                _____

5. I often see (they, them) in the cafeteria.                  _____

6. Don't lend money to (she, her).                             _____

7. There (isn't, aren't) one window in the room.               _____

8. I spend (a, an) hour on my homework every day.              _____

9. John sat down and (puts, put )his feet up on a chair.       _____

10. There (was, were) nobody in the office.                    _____

11. (Have, has) she many friends in the class?                 _____

12. He teaches (we, us) English.                               _____

13. Both doors (were, was) closed.                             _____

14. Last night we stayed at home and (watch, watched) television.   _____

15. John was absent (in, from) the lesson yesterday.           _____

16. They (studies, study) English every day.                   _____

17. How many English books (you have, have you)?               _____

18. (Was, were) you at the lesson yesterday?                   _____

19. He is (a, an) very old man.                                _____

20. Is John (a, an) American or a Frenchman?                   _____

21. My father usually (get, gets) up early every morning.      _____

22. What color (is, are) your shoes?                           _____

23. He is (a, an) honest man.                                  _____

24. Last night we (eat, ate) dinner at home.                   _____

31

**PAST TENSE OF VERBS - REVIEW:** Change from present tense to past tense; write correct form of the verb in the blank spaces.

---

1. We *walk* through the park every day.     (walked)

2. He is a good student.

3. He drinks coffee with all his meals.

4. They come to school by bus.

5. He needs a new suit.

6. He always talks to us in English.

7. We are good friends.

8. He has many friends here.

9. They have a new car.

10. He speaks Spanish well.

11. She and I are students in the same class.

12. He reads the newspaper every morning.

13. I buy all my clothes in that store.

14. He smokes very much.

15. We learn many new words every day.

16. The teacher asks us many questions.

17. Our lesson ends at two o'clock.

18. The weather is good.

19. Both windows are closed.

20. There is nobody at home.

21. He follows his brother everywhere.

22. He always sits in this seat.

# PAST TENSE OF VERBS - REVIEW (continued). Change from past tense to present tense; write correct form of the verb in the blanks at the right.

1. He often *came* to see us.    (comes)

2. They had many friends in our class.    _____

3. I bought all my books in the school book store.    _____

4. They usually spoke English with us.    _____

5. The teacher read many good stories to us.    _____

6. We always ate lunch in the cafeteria.    _____

7. They were good students.    _____

8. She was my teacher.    _____

9. I waited on the corner for them.    _____

10. He asked us many questions.    _____

11. I got up very early.    _____

12. She wrote many letters to me.    _____

13. He always put his books on this desk.    _____

14. He needed more lessons.    _____

15. The bus stopped on this corner.    _____

16. We were very busy.    _____

17. He liked to swim.    _____

18. She wanted to learn English.    _____

19. It was an easy exercise.    _____

20. There were many students absent.    _____

21. They always came to school on time.    _____

22. The child drank very much milk.    _____

**NEGATIVE FORM:** We learned earlier that with the verb *to be* we obtain the negative form by placing *not* after the verb. Likewise, with the auxiliary verbs *can, may, must, should,* etc., we form the negative simply by placing *not* after these auxiliaries. Examples:-

He can speak English.      She must go there.
He can *not* speak English.      She must *not* go there.

---

Change to negative form. In the blanks at the right, fill in the auxiliary verb followed by *not*. Also include the main verb of each sentence.

1. She can speak French well.      (can not speak)
2. He should speak Spanish for this lesson.      ------------
3. You may smoke here.      ------------
4. They may be very busy.      ------------
5. He must see her.      ------------
6. I can telephone to him later.      ------------
7. You should tell her all about it.      ------------
8. She must go today.      ------------
9. She can play the piano well.      ------------
10. You may open the window.      ------------
11. They should be back before noon.      ------------
12. He can do all of these exercises well.      ------------
13. John may go to the party with us.      ------------
14. You may wait here.      ------------
15. They can meet us later.      ------------
16. He should sit near the window.      ------------
17. We must tell John about it.      ------------
18. He can go with us to the movies.      ------------
19. You may sit here alongside of John.      ------------
20. We must do that again.      ------------

**QUESTION FORM:** We learned earlier that with the verb *to be* we form questions by placing the verb before the subject. Likewise, with the auxiliary verbs *can, may, must, should,* etc., we form questions by placing these auxiliary verbs before the subject.

He can speak English.        She must go there.
*Can* he speak English?      *Must* she go there?

---

Change to question form. Use blank spaces to write in the auxiliary verb followed by the subject of the sentence. Include the main verb.

1.  She can speak French well.                      (Can she speak) _____

2.  He should wait on that corner. _____

3.  You may smoke here. _____

4.  I can meet you at two o'clock. _____

5.  He must go out of town. _____

6.  She should tell Helen about it. _____

7.  She can go with us tonight. _____

8.  He may wait in Mr. Smith's office. _____

9.  We must explain it to him. _____

10. You may wait in his office. _____

11. They may sit here. _____

12. You should stay at home. _____

13. He can meet us after dinner. _____

14. He can swim very well. _____

15. You must write him a letter. _____

16. She can attend class tomorrow. _____

17. He can play the violin well. _____

18. They can speak Spanish well. _____

19. I can understand everything he says. _____

20. She can do all these exercises well. _____

35

**SIMPLE PRESENT TENSE; NEGATIVE FORM:** In the simple present tense, where there is no regular auxiliary verb, we must introduce special auxiliary verbs in order to form a negative. The auxiliaries which we use for this purpose are *do* and *does*. We use *does* for the third person singular; we use *do* for all other persons, singular and plural. The word *not* then follows these auxiliaries.

|  |  |
|---|---|
| I *do* not speak | we *do* not speak |
| you *do* not speak | you *do* not speak |
| he, she, it *does* not speak | they *do* not speak |

---

Change to negative form. Write the necessary auxiliary verb followed by *not* in the blanks at the right. Also include the main verb.

1. He studies in our class.      (does not study)
2. They go to the movies every night.
3. She comes to school by bus.
4. I know him very well.
5. It rains very often during the month of April.
6. The dog runs after the cat.
7. Our class begins at eight o'clock.
8. It ends at ten o'clock.
9. The buses stop on this corner.
10. We write many letters.
11. She speaks English well.
12. You walk to work every day.
13. They like to study English.
14. Helen lives in Chicago.
15. He works on Sunday.
16. I go to school by bus.
17. I always arrive at school on time.
18. We need more practice in English.
19. I understand him very well.
20. She gets up early every morning.
21. It snows very often during the month of January.
22. We study very hard.

**SIMPLE PRESENT TENSE; QUESTION FORM:** For the same reasons that we use *do* and *does* as special auxiliary verbs to form negatives in the simple present tense (See previous exercise), we use *do* and *does* to form questions in this tense. Again, as in the case of negatives, we use *does* as the auxiliary for the third person singular; we use *do* as the auxiliary for all other persons, singular and plural. To form a question, the auxiliary is placed before the subject.

| | |
|---|---|
| *Do* I speak? | Do we speak? |
| *Do* you speak? | Do you speak? |
| *Does* he, she, it speak? | Do they speak? |

---

Change to question form. Write the necessary auxiliary verb followed by the subject in the blanks at the right. Also include the main verb.

1. He comes to school by bus. _(Does he come)_
2. They speak Spanish well. _____
3. He gets up early every morning. _____
4. We eat dinner at home. _____
5. I like to study English. _____
6. He wants to learn English. _____
7. I prefer to study in this class. _____
8. He always talks to us in English. _____
9. They live near the corner. _____
10. He takes his car to work every day. _____
11. John smokes very much. _____
12. She dances well. _____
13. I know him very well. _____
14. You understand everything he says. _____
15. I get up early every morning. _____
16. He reads many English books. _____
17. We want to learn English. _____
18. They come to class early. _____
19. Mary always arrives at the lesson on time. _____
20. It rains very often during this month. _____
21. He eats lunch in the cafeteria. _____
22. They sell newspapers there. _____

37

**SIMPLE PRESENT TENSE; QUESTION FORM** (continued): Observe that even with some question words like *Why, Where, When, What time, How, How much,* an auxiliary verb must still be used in order to form a question in English.* Examples:

Where *does* John live?
Why *do* they live in that old house?

---

In the blanks at the right, write the necessary auxiliary verb *do* or *does* in order to complete the meaning of these present tense questions.

1. Where ............ Helen work? (does)

2. Where ............ you live?

3. What time ............ your lesson begin?

4. What time ............ you arrive at school every day?

5. How well ............ John speak English?

6. When ............ the next train arrive?

7. Why ............ they work so hard?

8. What time ............ you get up every morning?

9. Where ............ John eat lunch every day?

10. How much ............ it cost to go to Chicago by plane?

11. When ............ Mr. Smith expect to return?

12. How often ............ it rain during the month of April?

13. Where ............ you eat dinner every night?

14. Why ............ John walk to school alone every day?

15. Where ............ he go after the lesson?

16. Where ............ Mary and her sister live?

17. How often ............ you go to the movies?

18. What language besides English ............ your teacher speak?

19. How ............ you feel today?

20. What time ............ you go to bed every night?

21. Why ............ Helen want to learn English?

22. How many hours ............ you sleep every night?

* The verb *to be* is the only important exception to this rule. With the verb *to be*, as we have learned (See page 4), it is possible to form a question simply by placing the verb before the subject.

38

**PAST TENSE VERB *To Be*; NEGATIVE FORM:** The negative form of the past tense of the verb *to be* is obtained in the same way as the negative form of the present tense (See page 3), namely, by placing *not* after the verb.

He was *not* a good student.
They were *not* at home last night.

---

Change to negative form. In the blanks at the right, insert the verb of each sentence followed by *not*. Use the contracted forms *wasn't* and *weren't*.

1. John was in my class. _____ (wasn't)
2. We were very good friends. _____
3. The door was open. _____
4. The lesson was easy. _____
5. You and George were at the meeting. _____
6. There were many students absent from class. _____
7. There was a magazine on the desk. _____
8. We were students in the same class. _____
9. They were cousins. _____
10. Both doors were closed. _____
11. I was very hungry. _____
12. Miss Jones was our teacher. _____
13. The weather was very good. _____
14. It was a very nice day. _____
15. She was a good companion. _____
16. They were both Americans. _____
17. They were in Europe all summer. _____
18. I was busy yesterday. _____
19. He was a tall man. _____
20. We were dead tired. _____
21. It was a very cold day. _____
22. There were many new words in the lesson. _____

**PAST TENSE VERB *To Be*; QUESTION FORM:** We form questions with the past tense of the verb *to be* in the same way that we form questions with the present tense (See page 4), namely, by placing the verb before the subject.

> *Was* he a good student?
> *Were* they at home last night?
> Why *were* you absent from the lesson yesterday?

---

Change to questions. In the blanks at the right, write the verb followed by the subject.

1. He was an old friend. _____ (Was he)

2. They were busy all day long. _____

3. He was a very intelligent person. _____

4. There were many students absent from the lesson. _____

5. Both windows were open. _____

6. The door was closed. _____

7. They were in Europe all summer. _____

8. There was a book on the table. _____

9. We were both dead tired. _____

10. They are both Americans. _____

11. We were students in the same class. _____

12. The lesson was easy. _____

13. The teacher was very angry. _____

14. He and she were first cousins. _____

15. The exercises were difficult. _____

16. The man was a stranger to me. _____

17. There was a letter for you on the table. _____

18. It was a very rainy day. _____

19. There were many dark clouds in the sky. _____

20. There was a large rug on the floor. _____

21. I was angry with him. _____

22. You were late for your lesson this morning. _____

**PAST TENSE, OTHER VERBS; NEGATIVE FORM:** Although we form negatives with the past tense of the verb *to be* simply by placing *not* after the verb (See page 39), we must have an auxiliary verb in order to form negatives with all other verbs. In the simple past tense the auxiliary verb which we use for this purpose is *did*. *Did* is used as the auxiliary for all three persons, singular and plural.

|                       |                     |
|-----------------------|---------------------|
| I *did* not go        | we *did* not go     |
| you *did* not go      | you *did* not go    |
| he, she, it *did* not go | they *did* not go |

---

Change to negative form. In the blanks at the right, fill in the necessary auxiliary verb *did* followed by *not*. Also include the main verb.

1. He spoke to me about it yesterday. _(did not speak)_
2. She came on time to the lesson. ------------
3. We ate lunch in the cafeteria. ------------
4. I bought all my books in the book store. ------------
5. The child drank all the milk. ------------
6. She wanted to learn English. ------------
7. He needed more lessons. ------------
8. I waited for you on the corner. ------------
9. He read the newspaper this morning. ------------
10. We watched television last night. ------------
11. He had many friends in the class. ------------
12. He liked to swim. ------------
13. She put all her books on the table. ------------
14. I got up early this morning. ------------
15. John came with me to the lesson. ------------
16. He asked me several questions about it. ------------
17. We learned many new words yesterday. ------------
18. I wrote a letter to my sister. ------------
19. The bus stopped on this corner. ------------
20. We ate dinner at home. ------------
21. She sat alongside of me at the lesson. ------------
22. She got very sick during the lesson. ------------

41

**PAST TENSE, OTHER VERBS; QUESTION FORM:** Although we form questions with the past tense of the verb *to be* simply by placing the verb before the subject (See page 40), we must have an auxiliary verb in order to form questions with all other verbs. The auxiliary verb which we use for this purpose is *did*. (Compare similar use of *did* to form negatives—see previous exercise, page 41). *Did* is used as the auxiliary for all three persons, singular and plural. To form a question *did* is placed before the subject.

| | |
|---|---|
| *Did* I go | *Did* we go |
| *Did* you go | *Did* you go |
| *Did* he, she, it go | *Did* they go |

---

Change to question form. In the blanks at the right, insert the necessary auxiliary verb *did* followed by the subject. Also include the main verb.

1. He spoke to me about it yesterday.      (Did he speak)
2. She waited for us on the corner.      ------------
3. They wrote him several letters.      ------------
4. The bus stopped on this corner.      ------------
5. They had dinner with us last night.      ------------
6. She wanted to go with us.      ------------
7. He preferred to stay at home.      ------------
8. I knew him very well.      ------------
9. You got up very early this morning.      ------------
10. They came to school by bus.      ------------
11. I read about the accident in the newspaper last night.      ------------
12. They lived near us.      ------------
13. She spoke to them in Spanish.      ------------
14. We talked together for a long time.      ------------
15. He bought his car in New York City.      ------------
16. She put on her hat and coat.      ------------
17. It rained very hard last night.      ------------
18. He arrived late for the lesson.      ------------
19. She wrote him a letter from New York.      ------------
20. We ate dinner in a restaurant last night.      ------------
21. They sat near her at the lesson.      ------------
22. The lesson ended at eight o'clock.      ------------

**PREPOSITIONS:** In the blanks at the right, fill in the necessary preposition.

1. Sometimes I walk ............ school.  __(to)__

2. Do you take sugar ............ your coffee?  _____

3. The train for Chicago leaves ............ three o'clock.  _____

4. It arrives ............ Chicago at ten o'clock.  _____

5. What did you have ............ lunch?  _____

6. Our class begins ............ nine o'clock.  _____

7. I thanked him ............ the information.  _____

8. I spoke to him ............ the telephone yesterday.  _____

9. Tell me all ............ your trip to Washington.  _____

10. The teacher stands ............ the class.  _____

11. There is a blackboard on the wall just ............ the teacher's desk.  _____

12. February comes ............ March.

13. July comes ............ June.  _____

14. *Tall* is the opposite ............ *short*.  _____

15. They live in that house ............ the corner.  _____

16. I was late ............ my lesson this morning.  _____

17. John was absent ............ class yesterday.  _____

18. He put the stamp ............ the envelope.  _____

19. I like to travel ............ train.  _____

20. She often goes to the movies ............ us.  _____

21. He asked me ............ a pencil.  _____

22. She asked me all ............ my trip to Chicago.  _____

23. How many months are there ............ a year?  _____

24. The dog jumped ............ the fence.  _____

**PAST TENSE OF IRREGULAR VERBS** (continued): As we learned earlier (page 27), the past tense form of many common irregular verbs must be memorized. Here are more verbs of this class, with their corresponding past tense forms:

| | | |
|---|---|---|
| go — went | hear — heard | leave — left |
| ride — rode | feel — felt | costs — cost |
| tell — told | begin — began | stand — stood |
| see — saw | sell — sold | understand — understood |
| give — gave | know — knew | |

---

Change to past time. In the blanks at the right, fill in the past tense form of the verb of each sentence.

1. He goes to school by bus. _(went)_

2. I hear someone in the next room. _____

3. She feels very well after her operation. _____

4. We ride on the bus every day. _____

5. I often see him on the street. _____

6. The teacher tells us many interesting stories. _____

7. Our lesson begins at eight o'clock. _____

8. I know him very well. _____

9. The train leaves at ten o'clock. _____

10. This dress costs ten dollars. _____

11. She gives me many presents. _____

12. They sell many different things in that store. _____

13. Our teacher stands in front of the class. _____

14. I understand him when he speaks in English. _____

15. We sometimes see him in the cafeteria. _____

16. The tickets cost two dollars each. _____

17. He leaves home every morning at eight o'clock. _____

18. The movie begins at eight o'clock. _____

19. We go to the movies every Wednesday night. _____

20. She tells me the answers to all the exercises. _____

21. We often ride through the park on our bicycles. _____

22. At the end of the school year I sell all my books. _____

**VOCABULARY REVIEW:** Choose the correct word and write it in the blanks at the right.

1. A man *sees* with his (ears, eyes, nose, mouth).  ____(eyes)____
2. The past tense of the verb *to feel* is (fall, full, felt, feels).  _____
3. We *buy* stamps in a (restaurant, cafeteria, post office, mail box).  _____
4. We pronounce the word *comb* to rhyme with (come, thumb, home, some).  _____
5. The next to the last *month* of the year is (January, February, November, December).  _____
6. The opposite of *put on* is (put away, take off, stop, begin).  _____
7. Which one of these *past tense* forms do we pronounce as a word of only one syllable: *counted, painted, walked, wanted?*  _____
8. A man *hears* with his (eyes, ears, mouth, hands).  _____
9. Which of these do you *pay* on the bus (bill, rent, fare, tax)?  _____
10. Which of these do you wear on your *hands* (tie, shirt, gloves, socks)?  _____
11. The opposite of *push* is (open, close, put, pull).  _____
12. In the United States, the weather during the months of January and February is generally (warm, cold, hot, rainy).  _____
13. We pronounce the word *these* to rhyme with (this, nose, sneeze, police).  _____
14. The opposite of *cheap* is (poor, expensive, rich, new).  _____
15. Which letter of the word *answer* is silent (not pronounced)?  _____
16. Which letter of the word *walk* is silent (not pronounced)?  _____
17. Which one of these meals do we eat in the morning (breakfast, lunch, dinner, supper)?  _____
18. Which one of these meals do we eat during the middle of the day (breakfast, lunch, dinner, supper)?  _____
19. Which of these is a popular dessert in the United States (coffee, ham sandwich, apple pie, bread and butter)?  _____
20. The word *cafeteria* has five syllables. When we pronounce the word, on which syllable do we place the accent?  _____

45

**GENERAL REVIEW:** Choose the correct form and write it in the blank space.

1. (Did, does) John go with you to the movie last night?     (did)

2. Mary (get, gets) up every morning at seven o'clock.     _____

3. (This, these) books are new.     _____

4. Does a man (see, sees) with his eyes or with his ears?     _____

5. What time (do, did) you get up this morning?     _____

6. Do you want (a, an) apple?     _____

7. This is (a, an) hot day.     _____

8. She is (a, an) honest person.     

9. Where (you went, did you go) yesterday after the lesson?     _____

10. Mary likes (speak, to speak) English with the teacher.     _____

11. How many books (have, has) William?     _____

12. There (is, are) two men in Mr. Smith's office.     _____

13. Henry and John (was, were) not in class yesterday.     _____

14. I (eat, ate) lunch with Mary yesterday.     _____

15. Yesterday I (get, got) up at six o'clock.     _____

16. How many days (is, are) there in a week?     _____

17. They (go, goes) to the movies almost every night.     _____

18. I saw (she, her) in the cafeteria yesterday.     _____

19. She can not (speak, to speak )English well.     _____

20. I often meet (they, them) on the street.     _____

21. They (do, does) not study in our class.     _____

22. Mr. and Mrs. Smith (wasn't, weren't) at the meeting last night.     _____

23. (Do, did) you get to the class on time this morning?     _____

24. I (come, came) home very late last night.     _____

**VERB _To Have_; NEGATIVE FORM:** We learned earlier (page 6) that with the verb _to have_ we may form negatives in the present tense simply by placing _not_ after the verb. In present-day English, however, we generally treat _to have_ like all other verbs and use the auxiliaries _do_ and _does_ to form negatives.

> I _do not (don't) have_ a book.
> John _does not (doesn't) have_ many friends.

(In the past tense we always use the auxiliary verb _did_ to form negatives with _to have._ Examples: I _did not have_ an English lesson yesterday. John _did not have_ enough money to buy the tickets.)

---

Change to negative form, using the auxiliaries _do, does,_ or _did._ In the blanks at the right, fill in the necessary auxiliary verb followed by _not._ Also include the main verb.

1. Helen has many friends in our class.   (does not have) _____
2. I have a new fountain pen. _____
3. We have three English classes each week. _____
4. They have a new car. _____
5. We had a good time at the party last night. _____
6. I had an English lesson yesterday morning. _____
7. They had their vacation in June. _____
8. John has his vacation in July this year. _____
9. She has two brothers and one sister. _____
10. We have many new words to learn today. _____
11. Helen has a new hat. _____
12. You have a new fountain pen. _____
13. We have our English class in Room 203. _____
14. I had lunch in the cafeteria today. _____
15. We had dinner in a restaurant last night. _____
16. I have a bad cold. _____
17. John has a headache. _____
18. We have a new television set. _____
19. They have many friends in New York City. _____
20. That dog has a very long tail. _____
21. The teacher has red hair. _____
22. This book has a red cover. _____

47

**VERB *To Have*; QUESTION FORM:** We learned earlier (page 7) that with the verb *to have* we may form questions in the present tense simply by placing the verb before the subject. In present-day English, however, we generally treat *to have* like all other verbs and use the auxiliaries *do* and *does* to form questions.

*Do* you have a match?
*Does* John have many friends here?

(In the past tense we always use the auxiliary verb *did* to form questions with *to have*. Examples: *Did you have* an English lesson yesterday? *Did John have* enough money to buy the tickets?)

---

Change to question form, using the auxiliaries *do, does,* or *did.* In the blanks at the right, fill in the necessary auxiliary verb followed by the subject of the sentence. Also include the main verb.

1. He has many friends here.    (Does he have) _____

2. They had a good time at the dance last night. _____

3. You have a new hat. _____

4. She has two cousins in our school. _____

5. The teacher has red hair. _____

6. You have a headache. _____

7. We have our English class at ten o'clock. _____

8. I had lunch with Helen yesterday. _____

9. They have a new television set. _____

10. They had a very good time in Mexico last summer. _____

11. I have a bad cold. _____

12. Your book has a blue cover. _____

13. Helen has two brothers in the army. _____

14. He has his vacation in June this year. _____

15. Last year he had his vacation in August. _____

16. The room has many windows in it. _____

17. This book has many good exercises. _____

18. The child has both a cat and a dog. _____

19. We have many English books. _____

20. I had five dollars in my pocketbook. _____

**PRONUNCIATION - S and Z:** In English we sometimes pronounce the letter S like S and sometimes like Z. In the words *does, busy, his, goes*, for example, the letter S is pronounced like Z. In the words *class, bus, cost, miss*, the S is pronounced like S. The foreign student must naturally train his ear carefully to hear these differences and to pronounce such words correctly.

In the blanks at the right of the following words, write S or Z to show how the letter *s* is pronounced in each particular word.

| | | | | | |
|---|---|---|---|---|---|
| 1. | also | (S) | 23. | has | |
| 2. | busy | (Z) | 24. | closed | |
| 3. | this | | 25. | easy | |
| 4. | these | | 26. | dress | |
| 5. | those | | 27. | pens | |
| 6. | was | | 28. | eyes | |
| 7. | his | | 29. | books | |
| 8. | class | | 30. | nose | |
| 9. | goes | | 31. | knows | |
| 10. | some | | 32. | tennis | |
| 11. | first | | 33. | seat | |
| 12. | cousin | | 34. | bus | |
| 13. | tries | | 35. | news | |
| 14. | plays | | 36. | house | |
| 15. | movies | | 37. | raise | |
| 16. | case | | 38. | peas | |
| 17. | kiss | | 39. | business | |
| 18. | cats | | 40. | days | |
| 19. | dogs | | 41. | does | |
| 20. | puts | | 42. | comes | |
| 21. | likes | | 43. | eats | |
| 22. | brings | | 44. | rose | |

**VOCABULARY - OPPOSITES:** Write in the opposites of the following words:

| | | | | | |
|---|---|---|---|---|---|
| 1. | big | (little) | 25. | night | --------- |
| 2. | down | (up) | 26. | good | --------- |
| 3. | out | --------- | 27. | begin | --------- |
| 4. | stop | --------- | 28. | dirty | --------- |
| 5. | open | --------- | 29. | dark | --------- |
| 6. | under | --------- | 30. | late | --------- |
| 7. | last | --------- | 31. | empty | --------- |
| 8. | before | --------- | 32. | summer | --------- |
| 9. | husband | --------- | 33. | fast | --------- |
| 10. | find | --------- | 34. | east | --------- |
| 11. | shut | --------- | 35. | north | --------- |
| 12. | girl | --------- | 36. | easy | --------- |
| 13. | sister | --------- | 37. | sit | --------- |
| 14. | soft | --------- | 38. | sour | --------- |
| 15. | absent | --------- | 39. | young | --------- |
| 16. | woman | --------- | 40. | present | --------- |
| 17. | unhappy | --------- | 41. | dull | --------- |
| 18. | impolite | --------- | 42. | sick | --------- |
| 19. | wife | --------- | 43. | fat | --------- |
| 20. | daughter | --------- | 44. | pull | --------- |
| 21. | black | --------- | 45. | buy | --------- |
| 22. | sharp | --------- | 46. | close | --------- |
| 23. | married | --------- | 47. | single | --------- |
| 24. | sad | --------- | 48. | inside | --------- |

**PERSONAL PRONOUNS; REVIEW:** Write in the personal pronoun (*I, you, he, she, it, we, they, me, him, her, us, them*) which corresponds to the words in italics of each sentence.

1. *The book* is on the desk.                    (it)
2. *Mr. Smith* is in his office.                  _____
3. *John and his brother* are in the cafeteria.   _____
4. I saw *John and his brother* yesterday.        _____
5. Do you study with *George?*                    _____
6. Yes, I study with *George and his sister.*     _____
7. *This book* is new.                            _____
8. *Those books* on the table are old.            _____
9. We see *those people* on the bus every morning. _____
10. She has *her lesson* at one o'clock.          _____
11. I put *your hat and coat* on the chair.       _____
12. I put *your umbrella* in the corner.          _____
13. *Mary and I* like to study English.           _____
14. I saw *you with George* on the bus this morning. _____
15. *The maid* opened the door for me.            _____
16. He writes many letters to *his son.*          _____
17. *The weather* is very cold today.             _____
18. He put *his hat* on and left the room.        _____
19. *His son and daughter* live with him.         _____
20. I know *his son and daughter* very well.      _____
21. He always speaks to *Mary and me* in English. _____
22. *Mary and I* want to learn English well.      _____
23. *George* is a good student.                   _____
24. I like *George* very much.                    _____

51

**PLURAL FORM** (continued): (See exercise on page *11*)

a) Nouns ending in *y*, preceded by a consonant, change the y to *i* and add *es* to form the plural (Examples: city, cities; lady, ladies). If, however, the noun ends in *y*, preceded by a vowel, then only *s* is added (Examples: key, keys; monkey, monkeys).

b) Nouns ending in *f* or *fe* change the *f* to *v* and add *s* or *es* (Examples: wife, wives; leaf, leaves.

c) Although most nouns ending in *o* simply add *s* to form the plural, a few nouns ending in o such as *potato, tomato,* and *hero* add *es* (Examples: potato, potatoes; tomato, tomatoes).

---

In the blanks at the right of each word, write the plural form:

| | | | | | |
|---|---|---|---|---|---|
| 1. | tomato | (tomatoes) | 23. | leaf | ---------- |
| 2. | dish | ---------- | 24. | dress | ---------- |
| 3. | child | ---------- | 25. | sister | ---------- |
| 4. | city | ---------- | 26. | match | ---------- |
| 5. | book | ---------- | 27. | letter | ---------- |
| 6. | knife | ---------- | 28. | hat | ---------- |
| 7. | box | ---------- | 29. | man | ---------- |
| 8. | potato | ---------- | 30. | lunch | ---------- |
| 9. | class | ---------- | 31. | foot | ---------- |
| 10. | bus | ---------- | 32. | negro | ---------- |
| 11. | street | ---------- | 33. | echo | ---------- |
| 12. | exercise | ---------- | 34. | lady | ---------- |
| 13. | wish | ---------- | 35. | mouse | ---------- |
| 14. | copy | ---------- | 36. | wife | ---------- |
| 15. | pen | ---------- | 37. | boy | ---------- |
| 16. | key | ---------- | 38. | monkey | ---------- |
| 17. | church | ---------- | 39. | kiss | ---------- |
| 18. | hero | ---------- | 40. | face | ---------- |
| 19. | woman | ---------- | 41. | dog | ---------- |
| 20. | piano | ---------- | 42. | watch | ---------- |
| 21. | half | ---------- | 43. | tooth | ---------- |
| 22. | brother | ---------- | 44. | window | ---------- |

**FUTURE TENSE:** We use the future tense in English to express promise or determination.* We form the future with the auxiliary verb *will* and the simple (infinitive) form of the main verb—as follows:

| | |
|---|---|
| I will (shall) go | we will (shall) go |
| you will go | you will go |
| he, she, it will go | they will go |

In everyday conversation, we generally use the contracted forms *I'll*, *you'll* *he'll* etc. (Examples: *I'll see* you tomorrow. *We'll call* him later.)

---

Change to future time. Write the necessary auxiliary verb followed by the main verb of each sentence in the blanks at the right.

1. He studies in this class. _(will study)_
2. She works in this office. _____
3. You speak English well. _____
4. I come to the lesson on time. _____
5. They walk to their work. _____
6. He brings his friends to the lesson. _____
7. He opens the door for us. _____
8. He studies very much. _____
9. She brings all her books to the lesson. _____
10. He plays the violin well. _____
11. We carry all the small packages. _____
12. He speaks to us in English. _____
13. He writes a letter to his mother every day. _____
14. I bring you many presents. _____
15. She arrives at the lesson on time. _____
16. He has his lesson in this room. _____
17. They eat all their meals in the cafeteria. _____
18. The train leaves at eight o'clock. _____
19. You like that teacher very much. _____
20. She teaches us English and mathematics. _____

* To express simple future action, it is common practice in English today to use the form *to be going to* instead of the future tense (Examples: *I am going to* study French next year. We *are going to* take a walk in the park this evening.) See page 77 for further discussion of this form.

53

**VERB *To Be*; FUTURE TENSE:** We form the future tense of the verb *to be* in the same way that we form the future tense of all other verbs. We use the auxiliary verb *will* and to this auxiliary we add the simple (infinitive) form of the verb—as follows:

I will (shall) be      we will (shall) be
you will be          you will be
he, she, it will be    they will be

Again, as with all other verbs, in everyday conversation we generally use the contracted forms *I'll, you'll, he'll* etc. (Examples: *I'll be* here at two o'clock. *She'll be* back in an hour.)

---

Change to future time. For practice with contractions, use contracted forms only. Therefore, write in the blank spaces the contracted form of the subject and the auxiliary verb, followed by *be*.

1. He is in the cafeteria.      (He'll be) _____

2. They are on the second floor. _____

3. She is your new teacher. _____

4. He is a good student. _____

5. It is on the desk. _____

6. I am in the second class. _____

7. John is in Chicago. _____

8. He is a big boy. _____

9. This is your room. _____

10. We are very busy. _____

11. They are the best students in the class. _____

12. There is a table in the room. _____

13. She is very tired after each lesson. _____

14. They are at home. _____

15. The weather is very warm during this season of the year. _____

16. John is out of town all week. _____

17. I am glad to know her. _____

18. She is a very intelligent child. _____

19. We are both in the first class. _____

20. These exercises are easy for her. _____

**FUTURE TENSE; NEGATIVE FORM:** We form negatives in the future tense regularly, simply by placing *not* after the auxiliary verb.

| | |
|---|---|
| I will (shall) not go | we will (shall) not go |
| you will not go | you will not go |
| he, she, it will not go | they will not go |

The contracted form of *will not* is *won't*. In everyday conversation, we generally use this contracted form in all negative future sentences (Examples: I *won't see* her before tomorrow. She *won't take* her lesson today.)

---

Change to negative; use contracted forms only. In the blanks at the right, fill in the contraction *won't* followed by the main verb of the sentence.

1. He will see us at three o'clock.                    (won't see) _____
2. She will be back in an hour.                         _____
3. He will be the best student in the class.           _____
4. They will arrive on the two o'clock train.          _____
5. She will meet us here.                              _____
6. I will bring the medicine with me.                  _____
7. He will wait for us on the corner.                  _____
8. They will return sometime next month.               _____
9. She will help us with the work.                     _____
10. I will be back at three o'clock.                   _____
11. She will sign her name to the letter.              _____
12. He will eat in the cafeteria.                      _____
13. I will be able to meet you.                        _____
14. I will see you next Wednesday.                     _____
15. She will write to you soon again.                  _____
16. He will be in Washington next week.                _____
17. We will tell John about it.                        _____
18. He will be interested in the news.                 _____
19. You will like that picture very much.              _____
20. The weather will be warm tomorrow.                 _____

**FUTURE TENSE; QUESTION FORM:** We form questions in the future tense regularly, by placing the subject before the auxiliary verb.

| | |
|---|---|
| Will (Shall) I go | Will (Shall) we go |
| Will you go | Will you go |
| Will he, she, it go | Will they go |

---

Change to question form. Write in the necessary auxiliary verb, followed by the subject. Also include the main verb.

1. He will return next week.        (Will he return) _____

2. She will be back in ten minutes. _____

3. They will leave for California on Wednesday. _____

4. He will be out of town all month. _____

5. He will study at the University of Miami. _____

6. We will have our lesson at two o'clock. _____

7. He will be the best student in the class. _____

8. They will both make good progress. _____

9. John will be here in an hour. _____

10. We will write you a letter immediately. _____

11. They will wait for us on the corner. _____

12. The lesson will begin at ten o'clock. _____

13. It will end at eleven o'clock. _____

14. The meeting will last for more than an hour. _____

15. She will speak English well someday. _____

16. They will turn out to be good friends. _____

17. They will travel to both France and England during the summer. _____

18. There will be many students absent tomorrow. _____

19. You will have many exercises to prepare for tomorrow. _____

20. Henry will be late for the lesson. _____

21. There will be a short meeting of the students after the lesson. _____

22. Our teacher will be Miss Smith. _____

**VERB *To Be*; REVIEW OF PRESENT, PAST, AND FUTURE TENSES:**
Write the correct form (present, past, or future) of the verb TO BE in the blanks at the right.

1. John ............ in the cafeteria *now*.                          (is)
   a) John ............ in the cafeteria *yesterday*.         _____
   b) John ............ in the cafeteria *tomorrow*.          _____

2. They ............ in Mr. Smith's office *now*.                 _____
   a) They ............ in Mr. Smith's office *yesterday*.   _____
   b) They ............ in Mr. Smith's office *tomorrow*.    _____

3. She ............ sick *today*.                                         _____
   a) She ............ sick *yesterday*.                        _____
   b) She ............ sick *tomorrow*.                         _____

4. We ............ very busy *today*.                                _____
   a) We ............ very busy *yesterday*.                  _____
   b) We ............ very busy *tomorrow*.                   _____

5. Helen and Mary ............ in this class *now*.          _____
   a) Helen and Mary ............ in this class *yesterday*.  _____
   b) Helen and Mary ............ in this class *tomorrow*.   _____

6. There ............ many students absent *today*.          _____
   a) There ............ many students absent *yesterday*.    _____
   b) There ............ many students absent *tomorrow*.     _____

7. These exercises ............ easy for me *now*.             _____
   a) These exercises ............ easy for me *yesterday*.   _____
   b) These exercises ............ easy for me *tomorrow*.    _____

8. Mr. Jones ............ out of town *today*.                    _____
   a) Mr. Jones ............ out of town *yesterday*.        _____
   b) Mr. Jones ............ out of town *tomorrow*.         _____

9. I ............ very tired *today*.                                    _____
   a) I ............ very tired *yesterday*.                    _____
   b) I ............ very tired *tomorrow*.                     _____

## VERB *To Be* (continued)

REVIEW OF PRESENT, PAST, AND FUTURE TENSES; NEGATIVE FORM: Change the following sentences to negative form. In the blanks at the right, write the verb of each sentence followed by *not*. Use contracted forms only. In the future-tense sentences, be sure to include both the auxiliary verb and the main verb. Follow the examples.

1. He is in the cafeteria *now*.  (isn't)
   a) He was in the cafeteria *yesterday*.  (wasn't)
   b) He will be in the cafeteria *tomorrow*.  (won't be)

2. Mr. and Mrs. Reese are out of town *today*.  _____
   a) Mr. and Mrs. Reese were out of town *yesterday*.  _____
   b) Mr. and Mrs. Reese will be out of town *tomorrow*.  _____

3. You are very busy *today*.  _____
   a) You were very busy *yesterday*.  _____
   b) You will be very busy *tomorrow*.  _____

4. There are many students absent from class *today*.  _____
   a) There were many students absent from class *yesterday*.  _____
   b) There will be many students absent from class *tomorrow*.  _____

5. The weather is very good *today*.  _____
   a) The weather was very good *yesterday*.  _____
   b) The weather will be very good *tomorrow*.  _____

6. Both doors are closed *now*.  _____
   a) Both doors were closed *yesterday*.  _____
   b) Both doors will be closed *tomorrow*.  _____

7. John and I are in the same class *now*.  _____
   a) John and I were in the same class *last year*.  _____
   b) John and I will be in the same class *next year*.  _____

8. The lesson *today* is easy.  _____
   a) The lesson *yesterday* was easy.  _____
   b) The lesson *tomorrow* will be easy.  _____

9. I am very busy *today*.  _____
   a) I was very busy *yesterday*.  _____
   b) I will be very busy *tomorrow*.  _____

## VERB *To Be* (continued)

REVIEW OF PRESENT, PAST, AND FUTURE TENSES; QUESTION FORM: Change the following sentences to question form. In the blanks at the right, write the verb of each sentence followed by the subject. In the case of sentences in the future tense, write the auxiliary *will* followed by the subject and the main verb. Follow the examples.

---

1. They are in Mr. Smith's office *now*.       (Are they) _____

   a) They were in Mr. Smith's office *yesterday*.   (Were they) _____

   b) They will be in Mr. Smith's office *tomorrow*.   (Will they be) _____

2. The door is open *now*. _____

   a) The door was open *yesterday*. _____

   b) The door will be open *tomorrow*. _____

3. It is very cold *today*. _____

   a) It was very cold *yesterday*. _____

   b) It will be very cold *tomorrow*. _____

4. They are in Europe *now*. _____

   a) They were in Europe *last summer*. _____

   b) They will be in Europe *next summer*. _____

5. There are many new words in *today's lesson*. _____

   a) There were many new words in *yesterday's lesson*. _____

   b) There will be many new words in *tomorrow's lesson*.

6. John is in my English class *now*. _____

   a) John was in my English class *last year*. _____

   b) John will be in my English class *next year*. _____

7. The exercises *today* are very difficult. _____

   a) The exercises *yesterday* were very difficult. _____

   b) The exercises *tomorrow* will be very difficult. _____

8. We are tired after our walk in the park *today*. _____

   a) We were tired after our walk in the park *yesterday*. _____

   b) We will be tired after our walk in the park *tomorrow*. _____

9. The train is late *today*. _____

   a) The train was late *yesterday*. _____

   b) The train will be late *tomorrow*. _____

**REVIEW OF PRESENT, PAST, AND FUTURE TENSES** (continued)
OTHER VERBS. In the blanks at the right, write the correct form (present, past, or future) of the verb which appears in parentheses.

1. He (come) to school by bus *every day*.  (comes)

   a) He ............ to school by bus *yesterday*.  (came)

   b) He ............ to school by bus *tomorrow*.  (will come)

2. They (eat) in the cafeteria *every day*.  _____

   a) They ............ in the cafeteria *yesterday*.  _____

   b) They ............ in the cafeteria *tomorrow*.  _____

3. I (have) lunch with him *every day*.  _____

   a) I ............ lunch with him *yesterday*.  _____

   b) I ............ lunch with him *tomorrow*.  _____

4. We (arrive) on time for the lesson *every day*.  _____

   a) We ............ on time for the lesson *yesterday*.  _____

   b) We ............ on time for the lesson *tomorrow*.  _____

5. Mr. Smith (take) his car to work *every day*.  _____

   a) Mr. Smith ............ his car to work *yesterday*.  _____

   b) Mr. Smith ............ his car to work *tomorrow*.  _____

6. Helen (go) to the movies *every night*.  _____

   a) Helen ............ to the movies *last night*.  _____

   b) Helen ............ to the movies *tomorrow night*.  _____

7. He (wait) for me on the corner *every day*.  _____

   a) He ............ for me on the corner *yesterday*.  _____

   b) He ............ for me on the corner *tomorrow*.  _____

8. Our lesson (end) at three o'clock *every day*.  _____

   a) Our lesson ............ at three o'clock *yesterday*.  _____

   b) Our lesson ............ at three o'clock *tomorrow*.  _____

9. Mary and Helen (get) up early *every morning*.  _____

   a) Mary and Helen ............ up early *yesterday morning*.  _____

   b) Mary and Helen ............ up early *tomorrow morning*.  _____

# REVIEW OF PRESENT, PAST, AND FUTURE TENSES (continued)

OTHER VERBS; NEGATIVE FORM: Change the following sentences to negative form. In the blanks at the right, write the necessary auxiliary verb *(do, does, did,* or *will)* followed by *not.* Use contracted forms only. Also include the main verb.

---

1. He studies in our group.         (doesn't study)

   a) He studied in our group *last year.*     (didn't study)

   b) He will study in our group *next year.*    (won't study)

2. They live in Mexico now.

   a) They lived in Mexico last year.

   b) They will live in Mexico next year.

3. She comes here every afternoon.

   a) She came here yesterday afternoon.

   b) She will come here tomorrow afternoon.

4. I have my lunch at twelve o'clock every day.

   a) I had my lunch at twelve o'clock yesterday.

   b) I will have my lunch at twelve o'clock tomorrow.

5. We go to the movies every Wednesday night.

   a) We went to the movies last Wednesday night.

   b) We will go to the movies next Wednesday night.

6. Our lesson begins at two o'clock.

   a) Our lesson began at two o'clock yesterday.

   b) Our lesson will begin at two o'clock tomorrow.

7. John and Mary read the newspaper every morning.

   a) John and Mary read the newspaper yesterday morning.

   b) John and Mary will read the newspaper tomorrow morning.

8. You get up early every morning.

   a) You got up early yesterday morning.

   b) You will get up early tomorrow morning.

9. They sit in the park every afternoon.

   a) They sat in the park yesterday afternoon.

   b) They will sit in the park tomorrow afternoon.

# REVIEW OF PRESENT, PAST, AND FUTURE TENSES (continued)

OTHER VERBS; QUESTION FORM: Change the following sentences to, question form. In the blanks at the right, write the necessary auxiliary verb (*do, does, did,* or *will*) followed by the subject of each sentence. Also include the main verb.

1. She comes to school by bus *every day*.                          (Does she come?)
   a) She came to school by bus *yesterday*.                        (Did she come?)
   b) She will come to school by bus *tomorrow*.                    (Will she come?)

2. The train leaves at two o'clock every afternoon.                 _____
   a) The train left at two o'clock yesterday afternoon.            _____
   b) The train will leave at two o'clock tomorrow afternoon.       _____

3. Our lesson ends at one o'clock.                                  _____
   a) Our lesson ended at one o'clock yesterday.                    _____
   b) Our lesson will end at one o'clock tomorrow.                  _____

4. We eat dinner at home every night.                              _____
   a) We ate dinner at home last night.                            _____
   b) We will eat dinner at home tomorrow night.                   _____

5. The bus stops at this corner.                                    _____
   a) The bus stopped at this corner.                              _____
   b) The bus will stop at this corner.                            _____

6. I get up at seven o'clock every morning.                         _____
   a) I got up at seven o'clock yesterday morning.                 _____
   b) I will get up at seven o'clock tomorrow morning.             _____

7. She writes to her parents every day.                             _____
   a) She wrote to her parents yesterday.                          _____
   b) She will write to her parents tomorrow.                      _____

8. John goes to bed early every night.                              _____
   a) John went to bed early last night.                           _____
   b) John will go to bed early tomorrow night.                    _____

9. I wake up early every morning.                                   _____
   a) I woke up early this morning.                                _____
   b) I will wake up early tomorrow morning.                       _____

**ADJECTIVES—ADVERBS:** An adjective is a word which describes a noun (Examples: a *big* boy, a *soft* apple, a *careful* student). An adverb is a word which generally modifies or describes a verb. It tells *how* we do something. It generally ends in *ly* (Examples: He speaks *slowly*. She works *carefully*.) Many adverbs are formed simply by adding *ly* to the corresponding adjective.

| Adjective | Adverb |
|---|---|
| soft | softly |
| careful | carefully |
| beautiful | beautifully |

---

Write the correct form—adjective or adverb—in the blanks at the right.

1. She is a ............ (beautiful) girl.               (beautiful)
   --------
2. Mary plays the piano ............ (beautiful).        (beautifully)
   --------
3. This apple is ............ (soft).                    ----------
4. Miss Smith always speaks very ............ (soft).    ----------
5. John did the work very ............ (clever).         ----------
6. He is a very ............ (clever) boy.               ----------
7. Helen always prepares her lessons ............ (careful). ----------
8. She is an exceptionally ............ (careful) student.   ----------
9. My watch is ............ (slow).                      ----------
10. The old man walks very ............ (slow).          ----------
11. He does all his work ............ (quick).           ----------
12. This is an ............ (easy) exercise.             ----------
13. I can do this exercise ............ (easy).          ----------
14. I see him very ............ (frequent) in the cafeteria. ----------
15. He is a ............ (frequent) visitor in our home.     ----------
16. They are both ............ (serious) students.       ----------
17. They both study English very ............ (serious). ----------
18. John did the work very ............ (careless).      ----------
19. He is a very ............ (careless) workman.        ----------
20. That was a very ............ (foolish) thing to say. ----------
21. William acted very ............ (foolish) in that matter. ----------

## ADJECTIVES—ADVERBS (continued)

GOOD—WELL: Foreign students sometimes confuse *good* and *well*. *Good* is an adjective and therefore always modifies a noun. *Well* is an adverb and generally modifies a verb.

> She is a *good* student.
> She studies her lessons *well*.

Confusion occurs when we sometimes use *well* as an adjective. When used as an adjective, however, *well* has the meaning of "to be in good health". (Examples: Mary was sick but now she is *well*. John is *well* again after his long illness.)

---

Write *good* or *well*—whichever is correct—in the blanks at the right.

1. Mary is a very ............ student. (good)

2. She always prepares her lessons ............ (well)

3. John speaks English ............ ------

4. Our lesson today was very ............ ------

5. The movie last night was very ............ ------

6. William plays chess ............ ------

7. John always does his work ............ ------

8. Helen plays the piano ............ ------

9. She is also a ............ tennis player. ------

10. We will soon speak English ............ ------

11. I don't think she sings ............ ------

12. My new fountain pen writes very ............ ------

13. It seems to be a very ............ pen. ------

14. I was sick for several weeks but I am ............ now. ------

15. Henry can swim ............ ------

16. His brother is also a ............ swimmer. ------

17. Mary dances very ............ ------

18. Helen is also a very ............ dancer. ------

19. Everything William does he does ............ ------

20. Mr. Smith, our English teacher, also speaks French very ............ ------

21. But is he a ............ English teacher? ------

**MUCH—MANY:** We use *much* with singular nouns—with things of indefinite quantity which cannot be counted (Examples: You use *much* sugar in your coffee. She spends *much* time on her English.). We use *many* with plural nouns—with things which can be counted individually (Examples: I have *many* books. There are *many* students in our English class.)

In the blanks to the left of each word, write *much* or *many*, whichever corresponds correctly with the word.

| | | | | |
|---|---|---|---|---|
| 1. __(many)__ | windows | 23. _____ | coffee |
| 2. __(much)__ | smoke | 24. _____ | tea |
| 3. _____ | apples | 25. _____ | cups of tea |
| 4. _____ | space | 26. _____ | trouble |
| 5. _____ | people | 27. _____ | effort |
| 6. _____ | birds | 28. _____ | plants |
| 7. _____ | fruit | 29. _____ | flowers |
| 8. _____ | sugar | 30. _____ | strength |
| 9. _____ | rooms | 31. _____ | homework |
| 10. _____ | work | 32. _____ | friends |
| 11. _____ | students | 33. _____ | conversation |
| 12. _____ | windows | 34. _____ | news |
| 13. _____ | butter | 35. _____ | seats |
| 14. _____ | meat | 36. _____ | mistakes |
| 15. _____ | exercises | 37. _____ | vegetables |
| 16. _____ | time | 38. _____ | bread |
| 17. _____ | times | 39. _____ | letters |
| 18. _____ | snow | 40. _____ | salt |
| 19. _____ | money | 41. _____ | pepper |
| 20. _____ | rain | 42. _____ | mustard |
| 21. _____ cups of coffee | | 43. _____ | pens |
| 22. _____ | wind | 44. _____ | ink |

**NO—NOT:** Students sometimes confuse the use of *no* and *not* in English. As we learned in earlier exercises, *not* is the usual adverb used to modify the verb in all negative sentences (Examples: He does *not* speak English. She is *not* a good student.) In addition, *not* is used in the following ways:

(a) before a noun modified by an article—or a numeral

> *Not* a person spoke during the whole hour.
> *Not* one student attended the meeting.

(b) before the adjectives *much, many, any, enough. Not*, being an adverb, directly modifies these adjectives.

> *Not many* people attended the meeting.
> There was *not enough* time to telephone the police.

*No,* on the other hand, is an adjective. It is therefore used to modify nouns only. (Examples: He has *no* money and *no* friends. She spends almost *no* time on her English.)

---

In the blanks at the right of each sentence, write *no* or *not,* whichever is correct.

1. That room has ............ windows in it. (no)
2. He does ............ attend class regularly. _____
3. There are ............ boys in our English class. _____
4. Today is ............ Friday. _____
5. There was ............ much money in her purse. _____
6. ............ one girl wanted to dance with William. _____
7. We have ............ time to talk about that now. _____
8. ............ person in his right mind committed that crime. _____
9. There are ............ many students in the cafeteria now. _____
10. William has ............ English book. _____
11. Does John spend much time on his English? No, ............ much! _____
12. I have ............ time to study. _____
13. There are ............ many students absent today. _____
14. In fact, there are ............ students at all absent. _____
15. He has ............ money to spend on books. _____
16. He is ............ a good student. _____
17. There is ............ a really serious student in the whole class. _____
18. This exercise is ............ difficult. _____

**PAST TENSE OF IRREGULAR VERBS:** As we learned earlier (pages 27, 44), the past tense form of many common irregular verbs must be memorized. Here are more verbs of this class with their corresponding past tense forms.

| | | |
|---|---|---|
| become — became | lose — lost | catch — caught |
| break — broke | find — found | fight — fought |
| make — made | take — took | teach — taught |
| sing — sang | shake — shook | think — thought |
| ring — rang | bring — brought | forget — forgot |

Change these sentences to past time. In the blanks at the right, write the correct past tense form of the verb of each sentence.

1. She sings very well.      _(sang)_

2. It takes two weeks to go there by train. _____

3. She often brings her brother to the lesson. _____

4. I forget his name. _____

5. Mr. Smith teaches us both English and mathematics. _____

6. He loses much money at the horse races. _____

7. The bell rings at three o'clock every day. _____

8. The weather becomes very warm at this season of the year. _____

9. He makes many mistakes in spelling. _____

10. The teacher finds many mistakes in our compositions. _____

11. The boxers shake hands before the fight. _____

12. I catch cold very easily. _____

13. He fights with his brother continuously. _____

14. He thinks about his troubles continuously. _____

15. He becomes very tired at this time every day. _____

16. They take three English lessons each week. _____

17. The cat catches many mice. _____

18. John often forgets to bring his books to class. _____

19. Our telephone often rings during the day. _____

20. Mr. Smith makes much money in his business. _____

21. She always becomes sick in hot weather. _____

22. Helen and her sister both sing very well. _____

**PREPOSITIONS:** In the blanks at the right, fill in the preposition necessary to complete the meaning of the sentence.

1. He gave the money ............ his son.                                   (to)

2. The plane fell ............ the river.

3. She went to the store ............ some bread.

4. The animal jumped ............ a hole in the ground.

5. When did he leave ............ New York?

6. Did he go ............ plane?

7. She wants to hang the picture ............ the fireplace.

8. You can put your coat ............ that chair.

9. The airplane flew ............ the city.

10. Hurry or you will be late ............ the lesson.

11. Don't wait ............ him any longer.

12. He will remain in this country ............ next July.

13. Then he will return ............ his native country.

14. We must study from page 10 ............ page 12 for tomorrow's lesson.

15. He took a handkerchief ............ his pocket.

16. We walked ............ Fifth Avenue for about an hour.

17. The teacher sits ............ front ............ the class.

18. There is a blackboard on the wall ............ the teacher's desk.

19. There is a wastepaper basket ............ the teacher's desk.

20. Mr. Smith asked me all ............ my trip to Chicago.

21. The bus doesn't stop ............ this corner.

22. Did he leave a message ............ me?

23. I must look ............ the pencil which I lost.

24. Helen looked ............ me and smiled.

**VOCABULARY REVIEW; MISTAKES IN FACT:** In this exercise, correct the mistakes in fact by changing the italicized word or words. Write the correct word or words in the blanks at the right.

1. The last month of the year is *January*  (December)

2. The capital of the United States is *New York City*.  _____

3. The largest state in the United States is *California*.  _____

4. The smallest state in the United States is *Connecticut*.  _____

5. Ten plus four is *thirteen*.  _____

6. Ten minus four is *seven*.  _____

7. Ten times four is *thirty-five*.  _____

8. Winter begins officially on *November* 21st.  _____

9. Summer begins officially on *July* 21st.  _____

10. February comes *after* March.  _____

11. August comes *before* July.  _____

12. The opposite of EXPENSIVE is *new*.  _____

13. The opposite of EAST is *north*.  _____

14. There are *fifty* seconds in a minute.  _____

15. The past tense of SEE is *said*.  _____

16. The past tense of SIT is *set*.  _____

17. The plural form of THIS is *those*.  _____

18. The auxiliary verb which we use to form the future tense is *did*.  _____

19. A man hears with his *eyes*.  _____

20. Lemons are generally *sweet*.  _____

21. Before we go out, we usually *take off* our hat and coat.  _____

22. RIGHT AWAY means *later*.  _____

23. If I am THIRSTY, I want something to *eat*.  _____

24. We pronounce the word WALKED as a word of *two* syllables.  _____

## VOCABULARY REVIEW (continued)

Choose the correct form and write it in the blanks.

---

1. The opposite of *black* is (blue, yellow, green, white).  ___(white)___

2. The last month of the year is (November, December, October, July). ----------

3. The next to the last month of the year is (October, December, November, July). ----------

4. Which of the following is a fruit (horse, radio, pair, pear)? ----------

5. Which letter in the word *wrist* is silent (not pronounced)? ----------

6. Which letter in the word *knife* is silent (not pronounced)? ----------

7. Which of these past tense forms do we pronounce as a word of one syllable: *counted, asked, pointed, waited?* ----------

8. We pronounce the contraction *I'll* to rhyme with (will, mile, shall, girl). ----------

9. We pronounce the contraction *she's* to rhyme with (this, those, sneeze, miss). ----------

10. We pronounce the word *thumb* to rhyme with (room, soon, some, then). ----------

11. The word *newspaper* has three syllables. On which syllable do we accent the word—the first, second, or third syllable? ----------

12. The opposite of *lose* is (place, find, take, bring). ----------

13. We pronounce the word *crossed* to rhyme with (lose, loose, east, lost). ----------

14. *Presently* means (sometimes, very soon, much later, seldom). ----------

15. The past tense form of *can* is (may, could, might, should). ----------

16. Which of these do we use in a restaurant (blackboard, chalk, menu, eraser)? ----------

17. Which of these do we use when it rains (pencil, umbrella, fork, sweater)? ----------

18. Which of these verbs is in the past tense (saw, do, give, run, see)? ----------

19. Which of these verbs is in the present tense (saw, said, took, buy, taught)? ----------

20. Which of these verbs has the same form in the past tense as in the present tense (come, put, take, like, go)? ----------

**GENERAL REVIEW:** Choose the correct form and write it in the blanks at the right.

1. This car (belong, belongs) to Mr. Smith. _(belongs)_

2. Yesterday Mr. Smith (come, came) to school by bus. _____

3. What time (do, did) you get up this morning? _____

4. Mr. Reese is (a, an) Englishman. _____

5. John and I (was, were) both sick yesterday. _____

6. He spends (much, many) time on his English. _____

7. Helen (can speak, can to speak) French well. _____

8. John (have, has) many friends in this school. _____

9. Mr. Smith teaches (we, us) English and mathematics. _____

10. (Do, does) Mr. Smith speak Spanish well? _____

11. (No, not) one person in our class went to the party. _____

12. (No, not) many people attended the meeting. _____

13. John (catch, caught) cold at the beach yesterday. _____

14. Mary plays the piano (good, well). _____

15. She also sings (beautiful, beautifully). _____

16. John always prepares his lesson (careful, carefully). _____

17. (Tomatos, tomatoes) are my favorite vegetable. _____

18. The (leafs, leaves) fall from the trees in October. _____

19. We saw (they, them) on the bus yesterday. _____

20. I spoke to him (by, on) the telephone yesterday. _____

21. (Was, were) John absent from class yesterday? _____

22. (Do, does) John live near you? _____

23. (Do, does) you live near John? _____

24. (Do, does) John and you have much homework for today? _____

25. Mr. Smith is (a, an) old man.

71

**PRESENT CONTINUOUS TENSE:** To form the *present continuous tense* we use, as an auxiliary verb, the present tense of the verb *to be*, and to this auxiliary we add the present participle *(ing* form) of the main verb. Example:

I am working      we are working
you are working      you are working
he, she, it is working      they are working

We use the *present continuous tense* to describe an action which goes on *now* or *at the present moment.* (Examples: He *is talking* with her now. It *is raining.* They *are building* a new home.)

---

In the blanks at the right, write the present continuous tense form of the verbs in parentheses.

1. John ............ (prepare) his homework now.    <u>(is preparing)</u>

2. She ............ (wait) for me on the corner now.    _____

3. Look! It ............ (begin) to rain.    _____

4. The leaves ............ (begin) to fall from the trees.    _____

5. They ............ (take) a walk along Fifth Avenue.    _____

6. I ............ (begin) to understand English grammar now.    _____

7. We ............ (make) good progress in our courses.    _____

8. Listen! The telephone ............ (ring).    _____

9. We ............ (study) the exercise on page 72 now.    _____

10. The train ............ (leave) at this moment.    _____

11. Helen ............ (look) for her English book.    _____

12. Listen! Someone ............ (knock) at the door.    _____

13. Look! Mr. Smith ............ (walk) in our direction.    _____

14. My father ............ (read) the newspaper now.    _____

15. The wind ............ (blow) very hard now.    _____
16. The teacher ............ (look) directly at you.    _____

17. All the students ............ (laugh) at you.    _____

18. The bus ............ (stop) for us now.    _____

19. Mr. and Mrs. Smith ............ (build) a new home on First Street.    _____

20. Apparently Mr. Smith ............ (do) very well in his business now.    _____

## PRESENT CONTINUOUS TENSE (continued)

In the last exercise, page 72, we learned that we use the *present continuous tense* to describe an action which goes on *now* or at the *present moment* (Examples: He *is talking* with her now. It *is raining.)* Remember to distinguish in use between this *present continuous tense* and the regular *simple present tense*, which is used to describe an action which goes on every day or in general (Examples: He often *talks* with her. It usually *rains* very much during the month of April).

---

In the blanks at the right, write whichever is correct, the *present continuous tense* or the *simple present tense* form of the verbs in parantheses:

1. Our telephone ............ (ring) very often. — (rings)

2. The telephone ............ (ring) now. — (is ringing)

3. John always ............ (do) his lessons well. — _____

4. Look! It ............ (begin) to rain. — _____

5. The wind ............ (blow) very hard now. — _____

6. Mr. Smith ............ (smoke) very much. — _____

7. Look! He ............ (smoke) a cigarette now. — _____

8. Helen ............ (write) to her brother once a week. — _____

9. She ............ (write) a letter to her brother now. — _____

10. Look! Grace ............ (wave) to us from the other side of the street. — _____

11. Listen! Someone ............ (knock) at the door. — _____

12. We always ............ (have) a good time at Helen's parties. — _____

13. John ............ (have) his breakfast now. — _____

14. We ............ (have) English lessons three times a week. — _____

15. We ............ (have) an English class now. — _____

16. The bus always ............ (stop) at this corner. — _____

17. The bus ............ (stop) for us now. — _____

18. Look! George ............ (get) off the bus now. — _____

19. He always ............ (get) off the bus at this corner. — _____

20. Mr. and Mrs. Smith ............ (build) a new home on Second Street. — _____

73

# PRESENT CONTINUOUS TENSE (continued)

For further practice in the formation and use of the *present continuous tense,* change the verbs of the following sentences from simple to continuous form. In the blanks at the right, write the corresponding present continuous tense form of each verb. (Be sure, of course, that you understand the difference in meaning which occurs in each sentence when you make these changes. If not, see previous exercises, pages 72, 73.)

1. John *studies* in this class.                    (is studying)

2. He *goes* to the movies.                         _____

3. They *come* to visit us.                         _____

4. The wind *blows* very hard.                      _____

5. The leaves *fall* from the trees.               _____

6. The teacher *corrects* our compositions.        _____

7. John *prepares* his homework carefully.         _____

8. The bus *stops* at this corner.                 _____

9. He *drives* to work in his car.                 _____

10. The train *leaves* on time.                     _____

11. He *helps* Mary with her homework.              _____

12. He *eats* lunch in the cafeteria.               _____

13. He *does* his work well.                         _____

14. He *wears* a dark suit.                          _____

15. She *waits* for me on this corner.              _____

16. We *learn* English rapidly.                      _____

17. She *prepares* dinner for the whole family.     _____

18. She *wears* a yellow dress.                      _____

19. Helen *plays* the piano.                         _____

20. He *speaks* very slowly.                         _____

21. She *teaches* us English.                        _____

22. He *takes* cream in his coffee.                 _____

## PRESENT CONTINUOUS TENSE (continued)

NEGATIVE FORM: We form negatives with the *present continuous tense* regularly; that is, we simply put *not* after the auxiliary verb.

| | |
|---|---|
| I am *not* working | we are *not* working. |
| you are *not* working | you are *not* working |
| he, she, it is *not* working | they are *not* working |

Change the following sentences to negative form. In the blanks at the right, write the auxiliary verb of each sentence followed by *not*. Also include the main verb.

1. He is preparing his homework now.     (is not preparing)

2. The telephone is ringing.

3. The leaves are beginning to fall from the trees.

4. We are making good progress.

5. I am learning many new words.

6. They are building a new home on Second Street.

7. The bus is stopping for us.

8. I am having a good time.

9. She is having her lunch now.

10. He is reading the newspaper now.

11. They are watching television now.

12. He is doing well in his English.

13. They are traveling in South America now.

14. He is laughing at you.

15. The teacher is looking at us.

16. They are speaking English.

17. The wind is blowing hard.

18. The sky is getting dark.

19. I am getting hungry.

20. The weather is turning cold.

21. The watchman is turning on the lights.

22. She is taking off her hat and coat.

75

## PRESENT CONTINUOUS TENSE (continued)

QUESTION FORM: We form questions with the *present continuous tense* regularly; that is, we simply put the auxiliary verb before the subject.

| | |
|---|---|
| Am I working? | Are we working? |
| Are you working? | Are you working? |
| Is he, she, it working? | Are they working? |

Change to question form. In the blanks at the right, write the auxiliary verb followed by the subject of each sentence. Also include the main verb.

1. He is preparing his homework now.       (Is he preparing) _____
2. She is waiting for us on the corner. _____
3. The telephone is ringing. _____
4. The maid is cleaning the room now. _____
5. The mailman is delivering the mail now. _____
6. The birds are all flying south for the winter. _____
7. They are taking a walk in the park. _____
8. John is reading the newspaper. _____
9. Helen is preparing dinner for the whole family. _____
10. They are taking lessons in dancing. _____
11. The sky is getting very dark. _____
12. The wind is beginning to blow very hard. _____
13. William is becoming an expert in English grammar. _____
14. The teacher is talking with Mr. Smith, the principal of our school. _____
15. They are discussing the examinations. _____
16. Helen's family is moving to Chicago. _____
17. The bus is stopping for us now. _____
18. I am getting very hungry. _____
19. He is signing the letters now. _____
20. They are shaking hands like old friends. _____
21. John is being particularly friendly with him. _____
22. Mr. Reese is taking his son with him on his trip. _____

**FUTURE SUBSTITUTES; *TO BE GOING TO:*** Instead of the regular future tense, we often use the present continuous tense of *to go,* followed by an infinitive, to express intention or simple future action. Examples:

> I *am going to study* French next year.
> You *are going to be* late for class.
> He *is going to invite* Mary to the dance.

(Note: the word *going* has no particular meaning in such sentences; it is simply part of the grammatical phrase used to express intention or simple action in the future.)

---

In the blanks at the right, write the correct present continuous tense form of *to go,* followed by the infinitive of the verb shown in parentheses.

1. We ............ (study) English literature next year.   <u>(are going to study)</u>

2. He ............ (meet) us at eight o'clock.   _____

3. Helen ............ (buy) a new dress for the dance.   _____

4. We............ (go)* to Mexico on our vacation.   _____

5. They ............ (build) a new home on Front Street.   _____

6. George ............ (take) Grace to the dance tonight.   _____

7. We ............ (have) a picnic next Saturday.   _____

8. The paper says that it ............ (rain) tomorrow.   _____

9. I ............ (have) lunch with Helen today.   _____

10. She ............ (meet) me outside the cafeteria.   _____

11. We ............ (watch) television tonight.   _____

12. He ............ (study) engineering at college.   _____

13. John says that he ............ (be) a doctor when he grows up.   _____

14. The teacher ............ (give) us an examination on Wednesday.   _____

15. We ............ (travel) to New York by car.   _____

16. It ............ (be) difficult to reach him by phone.   _____

17. George ............ (teach) me how to swim.   _____

18. We ............ (go) to the beach every day next week.   _____

19. Mr. Jones ............ (give) a speech at the meeting tonight. _____

20. They ............ (get) married in June.   _____

21. It ............ (be) a hot day.   _____

22. I ............ (get) up early tomorrow morning.   _____

* Such a sentence is often shortened to "We are going to Mexico on our vacation."

77

**SHORTENED ANSWER FORM:** Very often in English, when we answer a simple, direct question, we use a shortened answer form which consists simply of the subject of the sentence and the auxiliary verb. Examples:

> Do you speak Spanish?
> Yes, I do.
> No, I don't.

> Can she play the piano?
> Yes, she can.
> No, she can't.

If the subject of the question is a noun, we generally replace this noun by a pronoun in our answer.

> Will Mr. Smith be here soon?
> Yes, he will.
> No, he won't.

> Did the sun shine yesterday?
> Yes, it did.
> No, it didn't.

---

To each of these questions give shortened answers, like those above. In each case, give, first, a positive answer; and, second, a negative answer. In your negative answers, use only contracted forms. Follow the examples:

1. Does Helen live near you? (Yes, she does—No, she doesn't)
2. Will you be in class tomorrow? _____
3. Will John be in class tomorrow? _____
4. Is it raining? _____
5. Is the telephone ringing? _____
6. Are there many students in your class? _____
7. Did you go to the movies last night? _____
8. Do you like to study English? _____
9. Are you going to the movies tonight? _____
10. Is John sick today? _____
11. Are both windows open? _____
12. Is this Mr. Smith's office? _____
13. Are we going to be late for class? _____
14. Can you meet me after the lesson? _____
15. Did it rain hard last night? _____
16. Will John and Mary be in class tomorrow? _____
17. Do you always go to school by bus? _____
18. Were you late for class this morning? _____
19. Does your dog bite? _____
20. Are you making progress in your English? _____

78

**ARTICLES:** (a) We use no articles in English before nouns which have a general meaning or represent a whole class of objects (*water, gold, air, truth*, etc.). If, however, these nouns represent some particular quantity or quality, then we use the definite article (Examples: *Gold* is an important metal. *The gold* in this ring is very old.) (b) We do not use articles before proper nouns, that is, before the names of persons, cities, streets, countries* etc. (Examples: Mr. Smith lives on Fifth Avenue. He will visit Italy, France, and Germany). (c) If, however, such proper nouns are not used alone, but are used as adjectives, then we use the definite article (Examples: *The Fifth Avenue buses* are often crowded. *The English language* is not difficult to learn.)

---

In the blanks at the right, write the article, when necessary. In those cases where no article is necessary, simply draw a line.

1.  ............ water in this glass is dirty.                                     (the)
    _____

2.  Everyone should drink several glasses of ............ water
    every day.                                                                    _____

3.  ............ water in many cities is not good.                                _____

4.  ............ New York City has a poor climate.                                _____

5.  ............ climate in New York City is not very good.                       _____

6.  Mr. Smith is from ............ California.                                     _____

7.  ............ California scenery is very beautiful.                            _____

8.  John lives on ............ Seventh Avenue.                                    _____

9.  I always take ............ Seventh Avenue subway to my
    work.                                                                         _____

10. ............ English is more difficult to learn than French.                 _____

11. ............ English language is difficult to learn.                         _____

12. We need ............ good light in order to study.                           _____

13. ............ light in this classroom is not good.                            _____

14. They recently discovered ............ oil in Cuba.                           _____

15. ............ oil which comes from Cuba is of high quality.                   _____

16. ............ Venezuela is a very rich country.                               _____

17. They say that ............ Venezuelan climate is excellent.                  _____

18. I like ............ sports of all kinds.                                     _____

19. ............ sport which I like best is football.                           _____

20. We plan to visit ............ Canada on our vacation.                         _____

21. We read a long article about ............ Soviet Union.                      _____

\* Exceptions: *The* United States, *The* Soviet Union, *The* United Kingdom.

79

**PAST TENSE OF IRREGULAR VERBS:** For further practice, here are some additional verbs with their past tense forms:

| | | |
|---|---|---|
| keep — kept | mean — meant | steal — stole |
| shut — shut | meet — met | drive — drove |
| cut — cut | sleep — slept | do — did |
| hit — hit | sweep — swept | blow — blew |

Change to past time. In the blanks at the right, fill in the correct past time form of the verb of each sentence.

1. I *meet* her in the cafeteria. _____ (met)

2. He *drives* to work in his new car every day. _____

3. The wind *blows* hard during the month of March. _____

4. We *sleep* late every morning. _____

5. The child often *hits* the dog with a stick. _____

6. She *sweeps* the whole house every morning. _____

7. John *does* his homework very carefully. _____

8. He *steals* only from very rich people. _____

9. The word *means* different things to different people. _____

10. The cook often *cuts* her fingers in the kitchen. _____

11. John always *shuts* the windows for the teacher. _____

12. The fence *keeps* the children off the lawn. _____

13. Mr. Smith *sleeps* only five hours each night. _____

14. George *does* me many favors. _____

15. They often *meet* in the park in the afternoon. _____

16. Mr. Smith *drives* his children to school every day. _____

17. During a hard storm, the wind often *blows* down some of our palm trees. _____

18. This knife *cuts* very well. _____

19. Children often *steal* the apples from our trees. _____

20. That light *hits* me right in the eye. _____

21. He *keeps* all his money in an old box. _____

22. The maid *sweeps* out the dining room before each meal. _____

**RELATIVE PRONOUNS *WHO* AND *WHICH*:** We use the relative pronoun *who* when we refer to a person; when we refer to a thing, we use *which*. (Examples: The book *which* is on the desk belongs to me. The man *who* telephoned is here to see you.)

In the blanks at the right, fill in *who* or *which*, whichever is correct.

1. The woman ............ is with him is his wife.   (who)

2. The book ............ is on the desk is a history book.

3. Is this the magazine ............* you want?

4. Mr. Smith, ............ lived in South America many years, speaks Spanish perfectly.

5. That is the pen ............ I was looking for.

6. The present ............ you brought me is very pretty.

7. Was it Mary ............ telephoned to me?

8. The girl ............ was here is my cousin.

9. Is that the bus ............ we must take?

10. The students ............ study hard make the best progress.

11. This is the class ............ I like best.

12. Is this the street on ............ you live?

13. Is this the pencil ............ you lost?

14. Both movies ............ we saw last week were very poor.

15. Our teacher, ............ is an American, has very clear pronunciation.

16. It was Mary ............ left the message for you.

17. That book ............ I read last night was very interesting.

18. It was I ............ telephoned to you.

19. Is that the car ............ you are going to buy?

20. The men ............ were here could not wait to meet you.

21. This is the office ............ he works in.

22. She is the clerk ............ sold me the article.

\* *Which* and *who* (whom), when direct objects of the verb, are often dropped from English sentences. Thus we may say, "Is this the magazine which you want?" or "Is this the magazine you want?" Both forms are correct.

**ADJECTIVES; COMPARATIVE DEGREE:** We form the comparative degree of most adjectives by adding *er* to the positive degree (Examples: tall—*taller*; cold—*colder*, etc.). If the adjective has more than two syllables, we generally form the comparative with *more* (Examples: difficult—*more difficult*; beautiful—*more beautiful*, etc.). The comparative form of adjectives is generally followed by *than*.

> John is *taller than* his sister.
> This lesson is *more difficult than* that one.

---

In the blanks at the right, write the comparative form of the adjectives in parentheses. Include the word *than*.

1. Helen is ........ (young) ........ Mary.    *(younger than)*
2. This book is ........ (interesting) ........ that one.
3. Oranges are ........ (sweet) ........ lemons.
4. The weather today is ........ (warm) ........ it was yesterday.
5. This exercise is ........ (easy) ........ the last one.
6. Helen is ........ (intelligent) ........ her sister.
7. The month of February is ........ (cold) ........ the month of March.
8. I am ........ (tired) ........ I was last night.
9. Our classroom is ........ (large) ........ your classroom.
10. This lesson is ........ (long) ........ the next one.
11. You seem to be ........ (busy) today ........ you were yesterday.
12. To me New York City is ........ (interesting) ........ Washington.
13. Park Avenue is ............ (wide) ............ Fifth Avenue.
14. This book is ........ (good)* ........ the last one I read.
15. The month of February is ........ (short) ........ the month of March.
16. The sea looks ........ (peaceful) today ........ it looked yesterday.
17. Your pronunciation is ........ (good) ........ John's.
18. Prices are ........ (high) this year ........ they were last year.
19. The Mississippi River is much ........ (deep) in some places ........ in others.
20. These flowers are ........ (beautiful) ........ those in your garden.

*The comparative form of *good* is *better*; the superlative form is *best*.

82

**ADVERBS; COMPARATIVE DEGREE:** We form the comparative degree of adverbs in the same way that we form the comparative degree of adjectives (See previous exercise), by adding *er* to the positive degree (Examples: soon—*sooner;* late—*later,* etc.). If the adverb has more than two syllables we generally form the comparative with *more* (Examples: rapidly—*more rapidly;* cleverly—*more cleverly,* etc.). Again, as with adjectives, the comparative form of adverbs is generally followed by *than.*

> He came *earlier than* we expected.
> He walks *more rapidly than* I.

---

In the blanks at the right, write the comparative form of the adverbs in parentheses. Include the word *than.*

1. We arrived at the party ........ (late) ........ they.     _(later than)_

2. We will get there ........ (soon) ........ you.     _____

3. He called ........ (early) ........ usual.     _____

4. He answered me ........ (quick) ........ I expected.     _____

5. She plays the piano ........ (good) ........ her sister.     _____

6. She also sings ........ (beautiful) ........ her sister.     _____

7. The train arrived ........ (late) ........ ever before.     _____

8. You can run ........ (fast) ........ I.     _____

9. We naturally speak much ........ (slow) ........ the teacher.     _____

10. John prepares his homework ........ (careful) ........ I do.     _____

11. Helen works ........ (hard) ........ the other students.     _____

12. I get up every morning much ........ (early) ........ John.     _____

13. You speak English much ........ (good) ........ I.     _____

14. He can do the work ........ (easy) ........ I.     _____

15. He returned ........ (soon) ........ we hoped.     _____

16. He goes there ........ (often) ........ I.     _____

17. Naturally, the old man walks ........ (slow) ........ his companion.     _____

18. They go to the movies ........ (frequent) ........ we.     _____

19. John drives even ........ (fast) ........ his father.     _____

20. Some people speak English ........ (clear) ........ others.     _____

**ADJECTIVES, SUPERLATIVE DEGREE:** We form the superlative degree of most adjectives by adding *est* to the positive degree. If the adjective has more than two syllables, we generally form the superlative with *most*. The definite article *the* always precedes the superlative degree.

| Positive | Comparative | Superlative |
|----------|-------------|-------------|
| tall | taller | the tallest |
| cold | colder | the coldest |
| interesting | more interesting | the most interesting |

In the blanks at the right, write the superlative degree of the adjectives in parentheses. Include the definite article *the*.

1. John is ............ (tall) boy in our class. <u>(the tallest)</u>

2. She is ............ (beautiful) girl in the school. _____

3. New York City is ............ (large) city in the United States. _____

4. Helen is ............ (intelligent) girl in our class. _____

5. William is ............ (good) student in our class. _____

6. The Mississippi River is ............ (long) river in the United States. _____

7. August is ............ (hot) month of the year in the United States. _____

8. This exercise is ............ (difficult) one in the whole book. _____

9. Park Avenue is ............ (wide) street in New York City. _____

10. Mr. Smith is ............ (busy) teacher in our school. _____

11. Grace is ............ (pretty) girl in our group. _____

12. Miss Reese is ............ (good) teacher of English in our school. _____

13. That store is ............ (large) store in town. _____

14. He is ............ (bad)* student in our class. _____

15. December is ............ (cold) month of the year in the United States. _____

16. He is ............ (young) boy in our class. _____

17. We visited ............ (expensive) night-clubs in town. _____

18. The Pacific Ocean is ............ (large) ocean in the world. _____

19. These exercises are ............ (easy) of all. _____

20. This is ............ (comfortable) chair in the room. _____

\* The comparative of bad is *worse*; the superlative is *worst*.

84

**VOCABULARY REVIEW; MISTAKES IN FACT:** In this exercise correct the mistakes in fact by changing the italicized word or words. Write the correct word or words in the blanks at the right.

1. The capital of the United States is *Philadelphia*.    (Washington)

2. The Atlantic Ocean lies *south* of the United States. _____

3. The opposite of CHEAP is *poor*. _____

4. In the word KNIFE, the letter *n* is silent (not pronounced). _____

5. The past tense form of CAN is *might*. _____

6. The past tense form of SPEAK is *spoken*. _____

7. There are *fifty* seconds in a minute. _____

8. On a watch or clock, the minute hand is *shorter* than the hour hand. _____

9. The English alphabet has *twenty-four* letters. _____

10. The superlative form of the adjective GOOD is *better*. _____

11. The first president of the United States was *Abraham Lincoln*. _____

12. There are *two* feet in a yard. _____

13. There are *fourteen* ounces in a pound. _____

14. Mexico lies *north* of the United States. _____

15. We pronounce the word STOPPED as a word of *two* syllables. _____

16. We pronounce the word WANTED as a word of *one* syllable. _____

17. We accent the word CAFETERIA on the *second* syllable. _____

18. April is the *fifth* month of the year. _____

19. To CALL UP someone is to *criticize* him. _____

20. A man sees with his eyes and hears with his *mouth*. _____

21. In the United States, the coldest season of the year is *summer*. _____

22. Abraham Lincoln was president of the United States during the *Revolutionary War*. _____

**PAST TENSE OF VERBS; REVIEW:** In the blanks to the right, write the past tense form of each of the following verbs.

| | | | | | |
|---|---|---|---|---|---|
| 1. go | (went) | 23. come | (came) | 45. want | (wanted) |
| 2. need | | 24. shut | | 46. give | |
| 3. take | | 25. shake | | 47. get | |
| 4. teach | | 26. sell | | 48. forget | |
| 5. tell | | 27. see | | 49. find | |
| 6. think | | 28. ring | | 50. fight | |
| 7. hear | | 29. ride | | 51. feel | |
| 8. write | | 30. read | | 52. eat | |
| 9. count | | 31. put | | 53. drive | |
| 10. have | | 32. visit | | 54. drink | |
| 11. prepare | | 33. study | | 55. do | |
| 12. work | | 34. live | | 56. cut | |
| 13. sweep | | 35. meet | | 57. cost | |
| 14. steal | | 36. mean | | 58. catch | |
| 15. stand | | 37. make | | 59. buy | |
| 16. sleep | | 38. lose | | 60. spring | |
| 17. paint | | 39. leave | | 61. break | |
| 18. push | | 40. know | | 62. blow | |
| 19. pull | | 41. keep | | 63. begin | |
| 20. sleep | | 42. be | | 64. become | |
| 21. sit | | 43. like | | 65. start | |
| 22. sing | | 44. hit | | 66. stop | |

**VOCABULARY REVIEW:** Choose the correct form and write it in the blanks at the right.

1. The opposite of *sharp* is (new, bright, old, dull).  _(dull)_
2. We pronounce the contraction *he'll* to rhyme with (fell, fill, feel, fall).
3. Which of these verbs is in the past tense (see, feel, fight, got, wait)?
4. Which of these verbs is in the present tense (gave, went, had, know, found)?
5. Which of these verbs has the same form in the past tense as in the present tense (go, hit, find, get, tell)?
6. Which *two* of the following words are both opposites of RIGHT (easy, wrong, straight, left, soon)?
7. *Right away* means (later, immediately, often, to the right).
8. To *pick out* something is to (need it, want it, choose it, lose it).
9. In which one of these words do we pronounce the letter *s* like a *z* (miss, this, is, pass)?
10. In which of these four seasons of the year does it rain most often in the United States (spring, summer, fall, winter)?
11. We pronounce the contraction *we're* to rhyme with (her, where, hear, wore).
12. The word *composition* has four syllables. On which syllable do we accent the word—on the first, second, third, or fourth syllable?
13. We often use the word *hard* as the opposite of (good, new, easy, fine).
14. The auxiliary verb which we use to form the future tense is (do, does, can, will, did).
15. Which of these past tense forms do we pronounce as a word of one syllable (wanted, needed, walked, pointed)?
16. Which of these past tense forms do we pronounce as a word of two syllables (pulled, asked, placed, talked wanted)?
17. Which letter in the word *knee* is silent (not pronounced)?
18. Which letter in the word *walked* is silent (not pronounced)?
19. *Loose* is the opposite of (big, find, open, tight).
20. The opposite of to *put on* is to (take away, take off, turn on, put away).

87

**PREPOSITIONS:** In the blanks at the right, write the correct preposition to complete the meaning of each of the following sentences.

1. The leaves fall ............ the trees in October. _(from)_

2. The bus is stopping ............ us now.

3. It is dark in this room. Please turn ............ the light.

4. Hurry! Helen is waiting ............ us.

5. All the students are laughing ............ us.

6. ............ present, he is the best student in the class.

7. Mary was absent ............ class yesterday.

8. What are they talking ............?

9. What is he laughing ............?

10. What are you thinking ............?

11. The beggar asked me ............ some money.

12. Hurry! We will be late ............ class.

13. She spends very much money ............ clothes.

14. This pen belongs ............ Mr. Smith.

15. I always go to school ............ bus.

16. I spoke to her ............ the telephone yesterday.

17. The airplane flew directly ............ our house.

18. The child ran and tried to hide ............ the tree.

19. He tried to explain ............ me what he wanted.

20. Helen is looking ............ the book which she lost.

21. Did you find ............ what John wanted?

22. He is leaving ............ New York on Wednesday.

23. Helen lives directly ............ the street from us.

24. In New York City the subways travel ............ the ground.

25. What is the difference ............ those two words?

88

**GENERAL REVIEW:** Choose the correct form and write in the blanks at the right.

1. Listen! Someone (knocks, is knocking) at the door. _(is knocking)_

2. (That, those) books belong to William. _____

3. Helen didn't like the movie (also, either). _____

4. I (can, could) not come to the lesson yesterday. _____

5. I saw (they, them) in the cafeteria at noon. _____

6. (No, not) one student was absent from class this morning. _____

7. Henry is taller (as, than) George. _____

8. This pen (belong, belongs) to Mr. Smith. _____

9. Does Henry (speak, speaks) English well? _____

10. Helen plays the piano very (good, well). _____

11. She also sings (beautiful, beautifully). _____

12. Do you want (a, an) apple? _____

13. We waited (a, an) hour for him. _____

14. We also waited (a, an) whole hour for him. _____

15. He spends (much, many) time on his homework. _____

16. (Was, were) Helen and her sister at the party last night? _____

17. He is the man (who, which) came to see you. _____

18. There (was, were) three students absent from class today. _____

19. John always prepares his lessons (careful, carefully). _____

20. She sings very (good, well). _____

21. He wants (go, to go) with us to the movies tonight. _____

22. It was difficult (learn, to learn) so many new words. _____

23. What time (do, did) you get up this morning? _____

24. He cannot (speak, to speak) English well. _____

**SOME - ANY**: We use *some* in positive sentences and *any* in negative sentences. Examples:

I have *some* money with me.
I don't have *any* money with me.

Choose the correct form and write it in the blanks at the right.

1. There aren't (some, any) chairs in the room. _(any)_
2. I saw (some, any) automobiles in the street. _____
3. I didn't see (some, any). _____
4. I have (some, any) new magazines with me. _____
5. He says that he saw (some, any) policemen on the corner. _____
6. I don't believe that he saw (some, any). _____
7. I don't have (some, any) time to study English. _____
8. I wrote (some, any) letters to them last night. _____
9. There are (some, any) flowers in the vase. _____
10. There aren't (some, any) flowers in this vase. _____
11. She says that she put (some, any) water in the vase. _____
12. I didn't see her put (some, any) water in the vase. _____
13. I gave John (some, any) money to buy the tickets. _____
14. He never makes (some, any) mistakes in grammar. _____
15. I learned (some, any) new words in English in today's lesson. _____
16. Maybe you learned some but I didn't learn (some, any). _____
17. There were (some, any) pretty pictures on the wall. _____
18. I didn't see (some, any) pretty pictures there. _____
19. She has (some, any) very pretty dresses. _____
20. However, she says that she doesn't have (some, any) pretty dresses to wear. _____
21. The teacher taught us (some, any) important grammar rules. _____
22. I didn't have (some, any) time to prepare my homework last night. _____

90

**SOMEONE - ANYONE, ETC.:** In the last exercise, page 90, we learned that in positive sentences we use *some*; in negative sentences we use *any*. Likewise, in positive sentences we use the derivatives of *some* (*someone*, *something*, *somewhere*, etc.); in negative sentences we use the derivatives of *any* (*anyone*, *anything*, *anywhere*, etc.)

I saw *someone* in the room.
I didn't see *anyone* in the room.

---

Choose the correct form and write it in the blanks at the right.

1. He didn't say (something, anything) to me about it.    _(anything)_
2. He told me (something, anything) about his trip.    ----------
3. There is (something, anything) wrong with this telephone.    ----------
4. I don't see (something, anything) wrong with it.    ----------
5. He lives (somewhere, anywhere) on Fifth Avenue.    ----------
6. I can't find my fountain pen (somewhere, anywhere).    ----------
7. I hear (someone, anyone) in the next room.    ----------
8. I don't hear (someone, anyone).    ----------
9. I saw (someone, anyone) in the hall with William.    ----------
10. There isn't (someone, anyone) at the door.    ----------
11. I was sure that I heard (someone, anyone) at the door.    ----------
12. He told me (something, anything) about the new teacher.    ----------
13. He didn't say (something, anything) to me about her.    ----------
14. I left my books (somewhere, anywhere) in this room.    ----------
15. Now I can't find them (somewhere, anywhere).    ----------
16. They say that there is (something, anything) wrong with the elevator.    ----------
17. There wasn't (something, anything) wrong with it a few minutes ago when I used it.    ----------
18. The doctors gave me (something, anything) for my cough.    ----------
19. I hear (somebody, anybody) in Mr. Smith's office.    ----------
20. I am sure that there isn't (somebody, anybody) there.    ----------
21. There isn't (somebody, anybody) who can help him now.    ----------
22. He says that he didn't speak to (someone, anyone) about it.

**NEW VOCABULARY - OPPOSITES:** In the blanks to the right, write the opposites of the following words.

| | | | | | |
|---|---|---|---|---|---|
| 1. | tall | (short) | 25. | sweet | (sour) |
| 2. | young | | 26. | few | |
| 3. | buy | | 27. | clean | |
| 4. | often | | 28. | absent | |
| 5. | beautiful | | 29. | push | |
| 6. | loose | | 30. | easy | |
| 7. | high | | 31. | narrow | |
| 8. | laugh | | 32. | remember | |
| 9. | sick | | 33. | lose | |
| 10. | inside | | 34. | low | |
| 11. | hard | | 35. | in front of | |
| 12. | dull | | 36. | under | |
| 13. | happy | | 37. | in | |
| 14. | push | | 38. | new | |
| 15. | wide | | 39. | good | |
| 16. | careful | | 40. | east | |
| 17. | empty | | 41. | sour | |
| 18. | white | | 42. | soft | |
| 19. | thick | | 43. | summer | |
| 20. | end | | 44. | late | |
| 21. | behind | | 45. | dark | |
| 22. | expensive | | 46. | down | |
| 23. | future | | 47. | sit | |
| 24. | heavy | | 48. | big | |

**PRONUNCIATION - SILENT LETTERS:** In each of the following words there is one letter which is obviously silent (not pronounced). In the blanks to the right of each word, write this silent letter.

| | | | | | |
|---|---|---|---|---|---|
| 1. | write | (w) | 22. | knee | (k) |
| 2. | listen | | 23. | walk | |
| 3. | knock | | 24. | talk | |
| 4. | knew | | 25. | kneel | |
| 5. | often | | 26. | Wednesday | |
| 6. | honest | | 27. | wrong | |
| 7. | whole | | 28. | should | |
| 8. | whistle | | 29. | wrist | |
| 9. | dumb | | 30. | guest | |
| 10. | half | | 31. | sword | |
| 11. | knife | | 32. | people | |
| 12. | could | | 33. | aisle | |
| 13. | Christmas | | 34. | guarantee | |
| 14. | island | | 35. | scissors | |
| 15. | answer | | 36. | scene | |
| 16. | doubt | | 37. | ghost | |
| 17. | guard | | 38. | wrote | |
| 18. | climb | | 39. | czar | |
| 19. | build | | 40. | pneumonia | |
| 20. | thumb | | 41. | knot | |
| 21. | honor | | 42. | guilty | |

**PAST TENSE OF IRREGULAR VERBS:** For further practice with irregular verbs, here are additional verbs of this class with their special past tense forms:

| | | |
|---|---|---|
| fly — flew | pay — paid | shoot — shot |
| grow — grew | run — ran | spend — spent |
| hold — held | say — said | throw — threw |
| hurt — hurt | send — sent | wear — wore |
| lend — lent | | win — won |

In the blanks at the right, write the correct PAST TENSE form of the verbs in parentheses.

1. Mr. Smith ............ (fly) to Chicago last week.    (flew) ⎯⎯⎯⎯⎯⎯⎯
2. Who ............ (lend) him the money to buy the car?    ⎯⎯⎯⎯⎯⎯⎯
3. The child ............ (run) and hid behind a tree.    ⎯⎯⎯⎯⎯⎯⎯
4. During our vacation last summer we ............ (spend) two weeks in Paris.    ⎯⎯⎯⎯⎯⎯⎯
5. These flowers ............ (grow) in my garden.    ⎯⎯⎯⎯⎯⎯⎯
6. The policeman ............ (shoot) the man in the arm.    ⎯⎯⎯⎯⎯⎯⎯
7. The teacher became angry and ............ (throw) our compositions into the waste-paper basket.    ⎯⎯⎯⎯⎯⎯⎯
8. Helen fell and ............ (hurt) her arm.    ⎯⎯⎯⎯⎯⎯⎯
9. I ............ (pay) two dollars for my English book.    ⎯⎯⎯⎯⎯⎯⎯
10. John ............ (say) that he was too busy to go with us.    ⎯⎯⎯⎯⎯⎯⎯
11. Grace ............ (wear) a long white dress to the party.    ⎯⎯⎯⎯⎯⎯⎯
12. They ............ (send) us several presents from Mexico last summer.    ⎯⎯⎯⎯⎯⎯⎯
13. The woman ............ (hold) the child's arm tightly as they crossed the street.    ⎯⎯⎯⎯⎯⎯⎯
14. We played tennis yesterday and John ............ (win) every game.    ⎯⎯⎯⎯⎯⎯⎯
15. She was born in Cuba but ............ (grow) up in the United States.    ⎯⎯⎯⎯⎯⎯⎯
16. The six policemen easily ............ (hold) back the crowd.    ⎯⎯⎯⎯⎯⎯⎯
17. John ............ (run) away from home when he was only ten years old.    ⎯⎯⎯⎯⎯⎯⎯
18. At the sound of the gun all the birds ............ (fly) away.    ⎯⎯⎯⎯⎯⎯⎯
19. We ............ (send) him two letters last week.    ⎯⎯⎯⎯⎯⎯⎯
20. Helen angrily ............ (throw) the money on the floor.    ⎯⎯⎯⎯⎯⎯⎯
21. The man ............ (hurt) himself badly when he jumped from the car.    ⎯⎯⎯⎯⎯⎯⎯
22. The child ............ (throw) the ball over the fence.    ⎯⎯⎯⎯⎯⎯⎯

**VERY - TOO:** Students sometimes confuse the use of *very* and *too*. *Very* means *much* or *in a large degree*. *Too* always suggests *something in excess, more of something than we need or can use*. Examine these two sentences:

The red book is *very* big, but it will go into my pocket.
The blue book is *too* big; it will *not* go into my pocket.

---

In the blanks at the right, write *too* or *very*, whichever seems to make the meaning of the sentence clearer.

1. I cannot wear this ring because it is ............ small for my finger.     _(too)_

2. This magazine is ............ large, but it will go into my desk.     _____

3. That other magazine, however, is ............ large to go into my desk drawer.     _____

4. That chair is ............ heavy for Mary. She cannot pick it up.     _____

5. It is a ............ heavy chair, but John is strong and can easily pick it up.     _____

6. You are speaking ............ fast. I cannot understand you.     _____

7. Our teacher speaks ............ fast, but I always understand her.     _____

8. This soup is ............ hot. I cannot eat it.     _____

9. The weather in Canada is ............ cold in winter, but Mr. Smith enjoys it very much.     _____

10. I cannot go out now. It is raining ............ hard.     _____

11. The sun was ............ hot for the child, and she became sick.     _____

12. It is ............ late, but if we hurry we can still catch the train.     _____

13. Mary says that she is ............ tired to go for a walk with us.     _____

14. The doctor says that Helen is still ............ weak to go to work.     _____

15. John studies English ............ hard and is making good progress.

16. Some of these exercises are ............ hard for me. I cannot understand them.     _____

17. This wine is ............ sour to drink. It will make me sick.     _____

18. These shoes are ............ small for me. They hurt my feet.     _____

19. It is ............ cold to go to the beach today. We will all catch cold.     _____

20. It was ............ cold, but we all went for a walk in the park.     _____

**PRONUNCIATION OF FINAL D AND T:** When we add the ending *ed* to regular verbs in order to form the past tense, we sometimes pronounce the final *d* as *d* and sometimes as *t*. For example, in the verbs *changed, learned, pulled, lived,* we pronounce the final *d* as *d*. In *asked, walked, passed, pushed,* we pronounce the final *d* as *t*. The reason for this change in pronunciation is the following: When we add *ed* to a word ending in voiceless consonant (*p, t, f, k, s,* etc.), the final *d* becomes unvoiced and is pronounced like *t*. When we add *ed* to a word ending in a vowel sound or in a voiced consonant (*b, d, v, g, z,* etc.), the final *d* remains voiced and is pronounced like *d*.

---

In the blanks at the right, write the letters T or D to show whether we pronounce the final *d* of each word as *d* or as *t*.

| | | | | | |
|---|---|---|---|---|---|
| 1. | pulled | (d) | 22. | crossed | |
| 2. | walked | (t) | 23. | earned | |
| 3. | passed | | 24. | entered | |
| 4. | washed | | 25. | stopped | |
| 5. | closed | | 26. | knocked | |
| 6. | changed | | 27. | saved | |
| 7. | used | | 28. | lived | |
| 8. | liked | | 29. | killed | |
| 9. | picked | | 30. | played | |
| 10. | mailed | | 31. | showed | |
| 11. | excused | | 32. | turned | |
| 12. | boiled | | 33. | dropped | |
| 13. | finished | | 34. | looked | |
| 14. | burned | | 35. | smoked | |
| 15. | filled | | 36. | wished | |
| 16. | poured | | 37. | rushed | |
| 17. | worked | | 38. | hurried | |
| 18. | studied | | 39. | placed | |
| 19. | talked | | 40. | jumped | |
| 20. | spelled | | 41. | remained | |
| 21. | thanked | | 42. | arrived | |

**CONTRACTIONS:** State the italicized words of the following sentences in contracted form. Write the contraction in the blanks at the right.

1. *I am* very busy today.                                    _(I'm)_

2. *You are* a very good student.                             _____

3. *He is* going to the movies with us.                       _____

4. *Helen is* also going with us.                             _____

5. *They are* both good students.                             _____

6. *I will* meet you at six o'clock.                          _____

7. *You will* get tired if you walk so far.                   _____

8. *He will* be back at six o'clock.                          _____

9. *John will* be here soon.                                  _____

10. *I have* a headache.                                      _____

11. *We have* much work to do today.                         _____

12. I *do not* know her well.                                _____

13. She *does not* speak English well.                       _____

14. He *did not* speak to me about it.                       _____

15. They *did not* arrive on time for the lesson.           _____

16. I *will not* be back until three o'clock.               _____

17. Helen *will not* be able to meet us.                     _____

18. I *can not* go to the party tonight.                     _____

19. She *is not* a good student.                             _____

20. They *are not* going to the party with us.              _____

21. Henry *was not* at the meeting last night.              _____

22. Helen and Mary *were not* at the meeting either.        _____

23. *There is* someone at the door.                          _____

24. *I am* not going to the movie tonight.                   _____

97

**CONTRACTIONS** (continued): The verb phrase of each of the following sentences appears in contracted form. For further practice with contractions, write the full form of each contraction in the blanks at the right.

1. He *doesn't* speak English well.      (does not) _____

2. I *can't* meet you after the lesson. _____

3. I *don't* know her very well. _____

4. He *won't* be back until later. _____

5. *John's* a good student. _____

6. *It's* a very hot day. _____

7. *She'll* be back in an hour. _____

8. *They're* the best students in our class. _____

9. *It'll* be easy for you to find him. _____

10. *She's* a very nice girl. _____

11. He *won't* be able to go with us. _____

12. Henry *wasn't* able to telephone to you last night. _____

13. *I'm* leaving on the three o'clock train. _____

14. *He's* going to study French next year. _____

15. I *didn't* have time to call you last night. _____

16. They *aren't* going to the movie with us. _____

17. She *isn't* a good student. _____

18. They *weren't* at the meeting either. _____

19. *There's* only one really good student in our class. _____

20. *There'll* be plenty of room for everyone. _____

21. He *hasn't* much money with him. _____

22. They *haven't* many friends in this town. _____

23. *You're* going to be late for class. _____

24. *You'll* be tired after so much work. _____

**CONTRACTIONS** (continued); PRONUNCIATION: Although contractions are not difficult to pronounce, the foreign student often mispronounces them because he considers them as two separate words loosely joined together. Actually, contractions are always pronounced as single words. In many cases they are pronounced as words of one syllable only.

---

Choose the correct word and write it in the blanks at the right.

1. We pronounce the contraction *I'm* to rhyme with (him, ham, time, some).  \_\_(time)\_\_

2. We pronounce the contraction *she's* to rhyme with (miss, place, sneeze, this).  _____

3. We pronounce the contraction *you're* to rhyme with (four, tore, fear, sure).  _____

4. The contraction *I've* rhymes with (leave, live, five, save).  _____

5. The contraction *they've* rhymes with (five, leave, save, live).  _____

6. The contraction *it's* rhymes with (eats, sits, sets, fights).  _____

7. The contraction *we're* rhymes with (were, wear, hear, her).  _____

8. The contraction *they're* rhymes with (fear, hair, wire, four).  _____

9. The contraction *I'll* rhymes with (will, mile, meal, call).  _____

10. The contraction *you'll* rhymes with (full, feel, jewel, fell).  _____

11. The contraction *he'll* rhymes with (well, will, hole, feel).  _____

12. The contraction *can't* rhymes with (paint, pant, faint, pint).  _____

13. The contraction *there's* rhymes with (wears, fears, pours, cheers).  _____

14. The contraction *they'll* rhymes with (wheel, well, jail, will).  _____

15. The contraction *he's* rhymes with (this, his, sneeze, police).  _____

16. The contraction *weren't* rhymes with (turned, current, learned, foreign).  _____

17. The contraction *it'll* rhymes with (will, little, tell, whistle).  _____

18. The contraction *we'll* rhymes with (well, fill, fell, feel).  _____

19. The contraction *she'll* rhymes with (shell, shall, will, meal).  _____

20. The contraction *we've* rhymes with (live, leave, left, love).  _____

99

**PREPOSITIONS:** In the blanks at the right, write the necessary preposition to complete the meaning of the sentence.

1. He placed the accent ............ the wrong syllable.    __(on)__

2. English grammar is very easy ............ me.    --------

3. The child ran and hid ............ a tree.    --------

4. This book belongs ............ William.    --------

5. He told us all ............ his trip to Europe.    --------

6. He will be in Europe ............ six months.    --------

7. I'll be back ............ ten minutes.    --------

8. I can study during the day but not ............ night.    --------

9. John prefers to study ............ the morning.    --------

10. He wants to take a trip ............ the world.    --------

11. We need more practice ............ conversation.    --------

12. He must spend more time ............ his English.    --------

13. They played a trick ............ him.    --------

14. Later they all laughed ............ him.    --------

15. He makes many mistakes ............ spelling.    --------

16. I saw the President ............ television last night.    --------

17. Helen wants to borrow some money ............ me.    --------

18. Shall I lend it ............ her?    --------

19. He arrived ............ Washington yesterday.    --------

20. The doctor gave me some medicine ............ my cough.    --------

21. We went ............ a walk in the park.    --------

22. She left a message ............ you.    --------

23. He will leave ............ Wednesday for New York.    --------

24. She will be very angry ............ you.    --------

**VOCABULARY REVIEW:** Choose the correct word or words and write it in the blanks at the right.

1. The opposite of *cheap* is (poor, expensive, new, old). _(expensive)_ _____
2. Which of these verbs is in the past tense: *see, fly, grow, ran, wear?* _____
3. We pronounce the word *said* to rhyme with (paid, head, sad, hid). _____
4. Which of these verbs is in the present tense: *threw, held, lent, shot, send?* _____
5. Which of these verbs has the same form in the past tense as in the present tense: *lend, send, hurt, win?* _____
6. *Pretty good* means (very good, not good, rather good, awfully good). _____
7. If you feel too hot, what do you do with your coat (put it on, take it off, pick it up, put it away)? _____
8. What is the superlative form of the adjective *good?* _____
9. What is the superlative form of the adjective *bad?* _____
10. Which one of these past tense forms do we pronounce as a word of only one syllable: *painted, counted, pushed, wanted?* _____
11. Which one of these past tense forms do we pronounce as a word of two syllables: *pulled, asked, thanked, waited, rained?* _____
12. Which of the following do we call a contracted form (you are, he is, we'll, they were)? _____
13. We pronounce the contraction *she'll* to rhyme with (tell, tall, still, feel). _____
14. In which of these can you travel fastest (street-car, bus, train, airplane)? _____
15. Which one of the following words is not spelled correctly: telephone, Wednesday, sylable, stopping, January? _____
16. Which letter in the word *wrist* is silent (not pronounced)? _____
17. Which letter in the word *ghost* is silent (not pronounced)? _____
18. In which of these words do we pronounce the letter *s* like z (kiss, does, this, ask)? _____
19. The word *alphabet* has three syllables. On which syllable do we accent the word—on the first, second, or third syllable? _____
20. The opposite of *often* is (never, seldom, frequently, sometimes). _____

**GENERAL REVIEW:** Choose the correct form and write it in the blanks at the right.

1. This is the book (which, who) I need.    (which)

2. He is much taller (as, than) John.

3. I didn't see (someone, anyone) in the room.

4. Listen! It (rains, is raining).

5. Yesterday he (feel, felt) much better.

6. They have (many, much) friends in Washington.

7. You use (much, many) sugar in your coffee.

8. He doesn't want to study French next year (also, either).

9. What time (will you, you will) be able to meet me?

10. We (are going, go) to school every day by bus.

11. They (have, are having) their lunch now.

12. (This, these) pencils belong to John.

13. Were you absent (in, from) school yesterday?

14. Let's not (to eat, eat) in that restaurant again.

15. The child (run, ran) from the room.

16. I'm sorry, but I (can, could) not come to the lesson yesterday.

17. Listen! The telephone (rings, is ringing).

18. Does he (makes, make) many mistakes in spelling?

19. What time (did, do) you get up this morning?

20. There (was, were) many students absent from class yesterday.

21. It is difficult (understand, to understand) him.

22. Helen always prepares her lessons (careful, carefully).

23. John speaks English (good, well).

24. I waited for him for (a, an) hour.

102

**ORDINAL NUMBERS:** The ordinal numbers are *first, second, third, fourth, fifth,* etc. The ordinal numbers are easy to form and to remember, in English. From *sixth* upwards, we simply add *th* to the corresponding cardinal number (Examples: six—sixth; seven—seventh; fourteen—fourteenth, etc.). We use the ordinal numbers frequently in English. We use them with all streets and avenues (Seventh Avenue, Sixty-first Street, etc.). We use them with dates (the 7th of October, February 12th, May 23rd) etc.

Using the blank spaces write the ordinal number which corresponds to each of the cardinal numbers below. In the second column of blanks, also write the abbreviation of each ordinal number. Follow examples:

|   |   | *Ordinal No.* | *Abbrev.* |
|---|---|---|---|
| 1. | one | (first) | (1st) |
| 2. | two | (second) | (2nd) |
| 3. | three | _____ | _____ |
| 4. | four | _____ | _____ |
| 5. | five | _____ | _____ |
| 6. | six | _____ | _____ |
| 7. | seven | _____ | _____ |
| 8. | eight | _____ | _____ |
| 9. | nine | _____ | _____ |
| 10. | ten | _____ | _____ |
| 11. | eleven | _____ | _____ |
| 12. | twelve | _____ | _____ |
| 13. | thirteen | _____ | _____ |
| 14. | eighteen | _____ | _____ |
| 15. | twenty | _____ | _____ |
| 16. | twenty-one | _____ | _____ |
| 17. | twenty-five | _____ | _____ |
| 18. | thirty | _____ | _____ |
| 19. | thirty-six | _____ | _____ |
| 20. | seventy-two | _____ | _____ |
| 21. | ninety-nine | _____ | _____ |
| 22. | one hundred | _____ | _____ |

**NEGATIVE FORM; GENERAL REVIEW:** In earlier exercises we studied how to form negatives in the various tenses; we are now ready to state certain general principles regarding the formation of negatives in English. (1.) With the verb *to be*, in the present and past tenses, we form negatives simply by placing *not* after the verb (Examples: He *is not* a good student. They *were not* in class yesterday.). (2.) If the verb phrase already contains an auxiliary verb, we form the negative by placing *not* after this auxiliary (Examples: You *may not* smoke here. He *will not* return until tomorrow.). (3.) If no regular auxiliary verb exists, as in the simple present and past tenses, we must supply an auxiliary verb in order to form a negative; the auxiliaries which we use for this purpose are *do* and *does* for the present tense and *did* for the past tense (Examples: He *does not* speak English. We *did not* go out last night.).

---

Change to negative form. In the blanks at the right, write the necessary auxiliary verb followed by *not*. Also include the main verb. (In the case of the verb *to be*, in the present and past tenses, write simply the verb of the sentence followed by *not*.)

1. They will study in our class.      (will not study)
2. She speaks English well.
3. She spoke to me in English.
4. She can speak English well.
5. He is an excellent student.
6. They went with us to the movies last night.
7. Henry was not in class yesterday.
8. They are having their lunch now.
9. It is raining hard.
10. The telephone is ringing.
11. The wind blows hard at this time of year.
12. I will be back in an hour.
13. He brought his sister to the lesson.
14. She plays the piano very well.
15. We must tell Mr. Smith about this.
16. You may wait here.
17. He wrote his composition in pencil.
18. It is a very warm day.
19. We were both absent from class yesterday.
20. I can meet you later.

104

**QUESTION FORM; GENERAL REVIEW:** In earlier exercises we studied how to form questions in the various tenses; we are now ready to state certain general principles regarding the formation of questions in English. (1.) With the verb *to be*, in the present and past tenses, we form questions simply by placing the verb before the subject (Examples: *Is he* a good student? *Were they* in class yesterday?). (2.) If the verb phrase already contains an auxiliary verb, we form the question by placing this auxiliary verb before the subject (Examples: *Can he* speak English well? *Will John* return soon?). (3.) If no regular auxiliary verb exists, as in the simple present and past tenses, we must supply an auxiliary verb in order to form a question. The auxiliaries which we use for this purpose are *do* and *does* in the present tense and *did* in the past tense (Examples: *Does Helen* study in your class? *Did you* go to the movies last night?).

---

Change to question form. In the blanks at the right, write the necessary auxiliary verb followed by the subject. Also include the main verb. (In the case of the verb *to be*, in the present and past tenses, write simply the verb of the sentence followed by the subject.)

1. They will return on Monday.                   (Will they return)
2. He left on the five o'clock train.
3. He is a good business man.
4. They visited us in our home last night.
5. He will be out of town for a week.
6. Someone is knocking at the door.
7. They were not in class yesterday.
8. John was sick yesterday.
9. We are going to study French next year.
10. It is going to rain.
11. There is someone at the door.
12. He spoke to her about it.
13. She speaks English perfectly.
14. Helen is one of his best friends.
15. They study in the same class.
16. She can meet us after the lesson.
17. We must write our exercises in ink.
18. The teacher gives us much homework.
19. They waited for us for an hour.
20. It is beginning to rain.

105

**PLACING OF ACCENT:** English is a language in which we strongly accent the main syllable of each word. Yet there are no rules concerning the placing of this accent. The student, therefore, must simply try to remember the correct pronunciation of each word.

In the blanks of the first column at the right, write the number of syllables which each of the following words contains. In the second column, write *1st*, *2nd*, *3rd*, or *4th* to show on which syllable we accent the particular word. Follow the examples.

| | | *No. of Syllables* | *Accented Syllable* |
|---|---|---|---|
| 1. | apartment | (3) | (2nd) |
| 2. | Canada | | |
| 3. | repair | | |
| 4. | banana | | |
| 5. | cafeteria | | |
| 6. | Mississippi | | |
| 7. | Chicago | | |
| 8. | popular | | |
| 9. | popularity | | |
| 10. | population | | |
| 11. | capital | | |
| 12. | telephone | | |
| 13. | tomorrow | | |
| 14. | president | | |
| 15. | preparation | | |
| 16. | prohibited | | |
| 17. | excused | | |
| 18. | finished | | |
| 19. | library | | |
| 20. | Saturday | | |
| 21. | Wednesday | | |
| 22. | nationality | | |
| 23. | language | | |
| 24. | holiday | | |

**REGULAR AND IRREGULAR VERBS:** We learned in an earlier exercise, page 25, that so-called "regular verbs" are those which form their past tense by adding *ed* to the present tense form. "Irregular verbs" are those which form their past tense in special or "irregular" ways—see page 27.

In this exercise, distinguish between those verbs which are *regular* and those which are *irregular*. In the blanks at the right, write *REG.* after all regular verbs and *IRREG.* after all irregular verbs.

| | | | | | |
|---|---|---|---|---|---|
| 1. | sit | (Irreg.) | 23. | stand | _____ |
| 2. | wait | (Reg.) | 24. | shut | _____ |
| 3. | bring | _____ | 25. | speak | _____ |
| 4. | count | _____ | 26. | meet | _____ |
| 5. | wish | _____ | 27. | talk | _____ |
| 6. | write | _____ | 28. | thank | _____ |
| 7. | win | _____ | 29. | make | _____ |
| 8. | wear | _____ | 30. | study | _____ |
| 9. | wash | _____ | 31. | stop | _____ |
| 10. | want | _____ | 32. | send | _____ |
| 11. | walk | _____ | 33. | shake | _____ |
| 12. | throw | _____ | 34. | run | _____ |
| 13. | think | _____ | 35. | raise | _____ |
| 14. | tell | _____ | 36. | put | _____ |
| 15. | wait | _____ | 37. | remain | _____ |
| 16. | visit | _____ | 38. | bring | _____ |
| 17. | use | _____ | 39. | protect | _____ |
| 18. | teach | _____ | 40. | pass | _____ |
| 19. | take | _____ | 41. | pick | _____ |
| 20. | swim | _____ | 42. | play | _____ |
| 21. | steal | _____ | 43. | buy | _____ |
| 22. | understand | _____ | 44. | cut | _____ |

107

**ABBREVIATIONS:** In the blanks to the right, write out the full form of each of the following abbreviations.

| | | | | | |
|---|---|---|---|---|---|
| 1. | 6 oz. | (six ounces) | 25. | 4 ft. | (four feet) |
| 2. | 1 lb. | _____ | 26. | St. | _____ |
| 3. | 1 mi. | _____ | 27. | Ave. | _____ |
| 4. | 7 A.M. | _____ | 28. | Blvd. | _____ |
| 5. | 6 P.M. | _____ | 29. | Rd. | _____ |
| 6. | .5 | _____ | 30. | Bldg. | _____ |
| 7. | ½ | _____ | 31. | Feb. | _____ |
| 8. | ¼ | _____ | 32. | Aug. | _____ |
| 9. | 6% | _____ | 33. | Dec. | _____ |
| 10. | #5 | _____ | 34. | sq. ft. | _____ |
| 11. | 68° | _____ | 35. | 1st | _____ |
| 12. | AC | _____ | 36. | 3rd | _____ |
| 13. | DC | _____ | 37. | 7th | _____ |
| 14. | etc. | _____ | 38. | Thurs. | _____ |
| 15. | 1 gal. | _____ | 39. | Wed. | _____ |
| 16. | TV | _____ | 40. | CBS | _____ |
| 17. | C.O.D. | _____ | 41. | NBC | _____ |
| 18. | qt. | _____ | 42. | N.Y. | _____ |
| 19. | pt. | _____ | 43. | Pa. | _____ |
| 20. | yd. | _____ | 44. | D.C. | _____ |
| 21. | in. | _____ | 45. | Md. | _____ |
| 22. | & | _____ | 46. | Mich. | _____ |
| 23. | Inc. | _____ | 47. | Cal. | _____ |
| 24. | 2 yrs. | _____ | 48. | Ill. | _____ |

**PREPOSITIONS:** In the blanks at the right, fill in the correct preposition to complete the meaning of the sentence.

1. He came to this country ............ 1945.                                    (in) _____

2. He goes to work ............ bus.                                             _____

3. They are ............ home today.                                            _____

4. There is someone ............ the door.                                      _____

5. He studied French ............ two years.                                    _____

6. I spoke ............ him about it.                                           _____

7. Please explain ............ me what you mean.                                _____

8. I looked everywhere ............ my book.                                    _____

9. We all went ............ a walk in the park.                                 _____

10. This chair is too heavy ............ me to carry.                           _____

11. He met us ............ the corner.                                          _____

12. We drove to school ............ John's new car.                             _____

13. He stole the money ............ his friend.                                 _____

14. The sun rises ............ the east.                                        _____

15. He makes many mistakes ............ grammar.                                _____

16. I often go to their home ............ dinner.                               _____

17. I'll be back ............ an hour.                                          _____

18. I am sure that I can finish this work ............ a few hours.             _____

19. Does the train always arrive ............ time?                             _____

20. He visited us ............ two weeks.                                       _____

21. John went to California ............ plane.                                 _____

22. He telephoned to me ............ the middle of the night.                   _____

23. He opened the door and walked ............ the room.                        _____

24. The airplane fell ............ the river.                                   _____

109

**VOCABULARY REVIEW; MISTAKES IN FACT:** In this exercise, correct the mistakes in fact by changing the italicized word or words. Write the correct word or words in the blanks at the right.

1. December is the *first* month of the year.    (last) _____

2. The next to the last month of the year is *October*. _____

3. The word CAFETERIA has *four* syllables. _____

4. We accent the word CAFETERIA on the *fourth* syllable. _____

5. The contracted form of WILL NOT is *willn't*. _____

6. The past tense form of CUT is *caught*. _____

7. The past tense form of HIT is *heat*. _____

8. The largest state in the United States is *Florida*. _____

9. Canada lies *east* of the United States. _____

10. The plural form of THAT is *these*. _____

11. There are *four* feet in a yard. _____

12. There are *six* quarts in a gallon. _____

13. There are *three* pints in a quart. _____

14. There are *fourteen* inches in a foot. _____

15. The second largest city in the United States is *Philadelphia*. _____

16. The largest river in the United States is the *Hudson River*. _____

17. The people of Brazil speak *Spanish*. _____

18. We pronounce the word THANKED as a word of *two* syllables. _____

19. The coldest season of the year in the United States is *autumn*. _____

20. If today is Tuesday, then the day before yesterday was *Saturday*. _____

21. If today is Tuesday, then the day after tomorrow will be *Friday*. _____

22. There are *fifty-six* weeks in a year. _____

23. In the United States we celebrate Independence Day on *May 30th*. _____

24. Thanksgiving Day always falls on a *Wednesday*. _____

110

**VOCABULARY REVIEW:** Choose the correct form and write it in the blanks at the right.

---

1. Which one of these verbs is in the past tense (see, bring, find, won, say)?

   (won)

2. Which one of these verbs has the same form in the past tense as in the present tense (win, hit, take, sit, see)?

   _____

3. A synonym for *plaything* is (lesson, toy, classroom, chalk).

   _____

4. To *call on* someone is to (see him, telephone him, visit him, like him).

   _____

5. If I am *tired out*, I am (rather tired, not tired, very tired, a little tired).

   _____

6. Which one of these words is not spelled correctly: daughter, grammer, interesting, secretary, Philadelphia?

   _____

7. In order to *sweep*, you need a (hammer, gun, stick, broom).

   _____

8. We pronounce the contraction *we're* to rhyme with (there, wear, near, fare, wire).

   _____

9. The opposite of *in front of* is (near, alongside, behind, between).

   _____

10. Which letter in the word *half* is silent (not pronounced)?

    _____

11. Which letter in the word *walk* is silent (not pronounced)?

    _____

12. In which of these words do we pronounce the letter *s* like *z* (kiss, visit, pass, ask)?

    _____

13. All of the following words rhyme except one. Which word does not rhyme with the others: lie, high, cry, fly, tea, buy?

    _____

14. All of these words rhyme except one. Which word does not rhyme with the others: fight, bite, right, height, weight?

    _____

15. A common synonym for *cent* is (nickel, dime, penny, quarter).

    _____

16. We pronounce the word *lose* to rhyme with (chose, loose, choose, blouse).

    _____

17. A synonym for *at last* is (later, once, finally, immediately).

    _____

18. *At once* means (later, one time, twice, immediately).

    _____

19. The opposite of *top* is (middle, end, bottom, side).

    _____

20. The eraser on the end of your pencil is generally made of (wood, cloth, steel, rubber).

    _____

**GENERAL REVIEW:** Choose the correct form and write it in the blanks at the right.

---

1. Look! That is John who (crosses, is crossing) the street. _(is crossing)_

2. Mr. Smith (comes, is coming) to school every day by bus. ----------

3. We (was, were) both absent from class yesterday. ----------

4. He doesn't (have, has) many friends in the class. ----------

5. There aren't (many, much) students in our English class. ----------

6. Your book is different (from, as) mine. ----------

7. Mr. Reese is (a, an) very old man. ----------

8. He is much younger (as, than) Mr. Smith. ----------

9. The weather today is (warmer, more warm) than it was yesterday. ----------

10. She speaks English almost (perfect, perfectly). ----------

11. He wants (me to go, that I go) with him. ----------

12. I didn't hear (someone, anyone) in the room. ----------

13. (No, Not) many students attended the meeting. ----------

14. He gave (her, to her) the money. ----------

15. He told (us, to us) the whole story of his trip. ----------

16. It was really (a, an) interesting story. ----------

17. Listen! I think it (begins, is beginning) to rain. ----------

18. He (does, makes) many mistakes in grammar. ----------

19. I don't know how old (is he, he is). ----------

20. I can do all of these exercises (easy, easily). ----------

21. He often (brings, is bringing) his sister to the lesson. ----------

22. (This, These) books belong to the teacher. ----------

112

**POSSESSIVE PRONOUNS:** The possessive pronouns in English are *mine,* *yours, his, hers, ours, theirs.* We use these possessive pronouns to avoid repetition.

> This book is *mine,* but that one is *yours.*
> These seats are *ours;* those seats on the other side of the room are *theirs.*

---

Change the italicized words in the following sentences to possessive pronouns. Write these pronouns in the blanks at the right.

1. This book is *her book.*                                        (hers)
2. These pencils are *my pencils.*                                 _____
3. This office is *his office.*                                     _____
4. These magazines are *our magazines.*                            _____
5. These cigarettes are *my cigarettes.*                           _____
6. Those cigarettes on the table are *your cigarettes.*            _____
7. These pencils are *their pencils.*                              _____
8. I think that this notebook is *your notebook.*                  _____
9. This newspaper is *my newspaper.*                               _____
10. This notebook is *her notebook.*                               _____
11. That hat and coat are *his hat and coat.*                      _____
12. This umbrella is *my umbrella.*                                _____
13. These seats are *our seats.*                                   _____
14. That pair of scissors is *her pair of scissors.*              _____
15. This classroom is *our classroom.*                            _____
16. That classroom on the other side of the hall is *your classroom.* _____
17. These books are *John's and Mary's books.*                    _____
18. Those books over there on the table are *my books.*           _____
19. Is this pen *your pen?*                                        _____
20. No, it is not *my pen;* it is John's.                         _____
21. Is this package of cigarettes *your package of cigarettes?*  _____
22. This package of cigarettes is *his package of cigarettes.*   _____

113

**REFLEXIVE PRONOUNS:** The reflexive pronouns are *myself, yourself, himself, herself, itself, ourselves, yourselves, themselves*. We use reflexive pronouns in English in two ways: (1) reflexively, to refer to the subject of the sentence and (2) emphatically, to give emphasis to some particular person or thing. Examples:

| (Reflexive use) | The girl burned *herself* on the stove.<br>The man shot *himself*. |
| (Emphatic use) | I *myself* will do the work.<br>Helen *herself* will telephone to you. |

---

In the blanks at the right, write the correct reflexive pronoun.

1. John shaves ............ every morning.     _(himself)_

2. Mary hurt ............ when she fell.     _____

3. I ............ will prepare lunch for everybody.     _____

4. Mary looked at ............ in the mirror.     _____

5. We enjoyed ............ at the party last night.     _____

6. The poor woman shot .............     _____

7. Be careful! You will cut ............ with that knife.     _____

8. The dog hurt ............ when it jumped over the fence.     _____

9. The child burned ............ on the hot stove.     _____

10. My young son can dress ............ very well.     _____

11. Can your little daughter dress ............ yet?     _____

12. I cut ............ yesterday on a piece of glass.     _____

13. Did you enjoy ............ at John's party last night?     _____

14. The President ............ will deliver the principal address.     _____

15. That horse will hurt ............ if it falls in that hole.     _____

16. We ............ heard John shout at the teacher.     _____

17. She says that she ............ will return the book to you.     _____

18. I enjoyed ............ very much at the opera last night.     _____

19. Mary says that she also enjoyed .............     _____

20. The soldier shot ............ with his rifle.     _____

## REFLEXIVE PRONOUNS (continued)

We often use reflexive pronouns idiomatically in English with the preposition *by* to give the meaning of *alone*. Examples:

> I went to the movies last night *by myself.*
> The old man lives *by himself* in a small apartment.

---

In place of the word *alone*, substitute the preposition *by* and a reflexive pronoun. In the blanks at the right, write *by* followed by the correct reflexive pronoun.

1. She went for a walk in the park *alone.*          (by herself)

2. I don't like to study *alone.*

3. He eats lunch every day in the cafeteria *alone.*

4. Do you like to eat *alone?*

5. The two boys will study *alone* in a special group.

6. Mary and I will also study *alone* in a separate group.

7. The old woman lives *alone* in a furnished room.

8. The dog found its way home *alone.*

9. He works *alone* in a small office.

10. He often goes for a walk in the park *alone.*

11. Do you like to go to the movies *alone?*

12. She did all the work *alone.*

13. He plans to go to Europe next summer *alone.*

14. The boys study *alone* in one group.

15. The girls study *alone* in another group.

16. I don't want to go to the theater *alone.*

17. Some people like to go to the theater *alone,* but I don't.

18. The servants eat *alone* in a special room.

19. John sat *alone* in a corner all evening long.

20. We plan to decorate the apartment *alone,* without help from anyone.

**PRESENT PERFECT TENSE:** To form the *present perfect tense* in English, we use the verb *have* as an auxiliary, and to this auxiliary we add the past participle of the main verb. (All past participles of regular verbs end in *ed* and are the same as the past tense form; for past participles of irregular verbs, see Appendix.)

| | |
|---|---|
| I have worked | we have worked |
| you have worked | you have worked |
| he, she, it has worked | they have worked |

We use the *present perfect tense* to describe an action which took place at some indefinite time in the past (Examples: I *have read* that book. He *has visited* us many times.)

---

In the blanks at the right, fill in the *present perfect tense* of the verbs in parentheses:

1. He ............ (spoke) to me about it many times.  (has spoken)
2. They already ............ (finish) their dinner.  ----------
3. I ............ (be) in Washington several times.  ----------
4. I ............ (hear) her sing once or twice.  ----------
5. They ............ (be) good friends for years.  ----------
6. We ............ (learn) many new words.  ----------
7. I ............ (lose) my copybook.  ----------
8. She ............ (study) that same exercise five or six times.  ----------
9. They ............ (clean) the house from top to bottom.  ----------
10. They ............ (give) up their home in the country.  ----------
11. She ............ (be) late for class many times.  ----------
12. We ............ (drive) to New York from Miami many times.  ----------
13. He ............ (make) and lost several fortunes.  ----------
14. The police ............ (captured) the thief at last.  ----------
15. Mr. Smith ............ (teach) many students to speak English.  ----------
16. I ............ (see) that same movie three times.  ----------
17. He ............ (lend) me money several times in the past.  ----------
18. I ............ (read) that novel several times.  ----------
19. Summer ............ (come) and gone already.  ----------
20. I ............ (speak) to Mr. Reese about that matter.  ----------

116

## PRESENT PERFECT TENSE (continued)

We also use the present perfect tense to describe an action which began in the past and which continues up to the present time. Examples:

> He *has worked* here for five years.
> They *have lived* here since 1954.

Notice the difference in meaning between the following two sentences; note that the first sentence is in the past tense and the second is in the present perfect tense:

> They *lived* here for two years—in 1948 and 1949.
> They *have lived* here for two years (They are still living here).

In the blanks at the right, fill in the correct tense *(past tense* or *present perfect tense)* according to the meaning of the sentence.

1. We are now living on 72nd Street where we ............ (live) for almost five years. **(have lived)** _____
2. From 1945 to 1950 we ............ (live) on 96th Street. _____
3. William ............ (study) French in Paris many years ago. _____
4. John is now in the hospital. He ............ (be) there for three weeks. _____
5. The First World War ............ (begin) in 1914 and ended in 1918. _____
6. I am now studying English. I ............ (study) for almost two years. _____
7. Helen ............ (study) Spanish when she was in high school. _____
8. It is natural that George speaks German well because he ............ (speak) it all his life. _____
9. Mr. Smith ............ (be) our teacher since January. _____
10. We ............ (be) in California last winter. _____
11. Mr. and Mrs. Jones now live in California. They ............ (live) there since 1949. _____
12. Before he came to the United States, Henry ............ (live) for two years in Venezuela. _____
13. He ............ (start) to study English as soon as he came to the United States. _____
14. He ............ (study) English continuously since then. _____
15. John and I are good friends. In fact, we ............ (be) friends for more than ten years. _____
16. We ............ (become) friends while we were students in the university. _____
17. Dr. Smith ............ (be) our family doctor ever since we first moved to this town. _____
18. My present automobile is a Buick. I ............ (have) it for three years. _____
19. My last car was a Chevrolet. I ............ (have) it for four years. _____
20. I ............ (see) Helen just a few minutes ago. _____

117

**PRESENT PERFECT TENSE; NEGATIVE FORM:** We form negatives with the *present perfect tense* in the usual way; that is, since a regular auxiliary verb forms part of the tense, we simply place *not* after this auxiliary verb. Examples:

> They *have not* returned yet.
> She *has not* felt well for a long time.

---

Change to negative form. In the blanks at the right, write the auxiliary verb followed by *not*. Also include the main verb.

1. We have been good friends for years.       (have not been) _____

2. She has felt well recently.       _____

3. He has worked here for about five years.       _____

4. I have read that story.       _____

5. He has studied English for many years.       _____

6. He has left for Chicago.       _____

7. The lesson has begun.       _____

8. She has always been the best student in the class.       _____

9. I have found my fountain pen.       _____

10. I have spoken to him about it many times.       _____

11. We have known each other a long time.       _____

12. He has been head of that department for two years.       _____

13. She has always been a very serious student.       _____

14. Helen has been sick for a long time.       _____

15. They have been in Europe since last January.       _____

16. We have lived in this house for ten years.       _____

17. He has been very kind to her.       _____

18. John and Mary have been absent from class all week.       _____

19. You have made this same mistake before.       _____

20. I have had time to do it.       _____

21. I have known him for a long time.       _____

22. He has mentioned it to me.       _____

**PRESENT PERFECT TENSE; QUESTION FORM:** We form questions with the *present perfect tense* in the usual way; that is, since a regular auxiliary verb forms part of the tense, we simply place this auxiliary verb before the subject. Examples:

*Has he* worked there a long time?
*Have you* ever been in California?
How long *has she* studied English?

---

Change to question form. Write the auxiliary verb followed by the subject of the sentence in the blanks at the right. Also include the main verb.

1. He has studied English for many years. (Has he studied)
2. They have known each other for a long time. _____
3. I have already seen that movie. _____
4. He has been in this class since January. _____
5. They have lived there since before the war. _____
6. Helen has always been the best student in the class. _____
7. They have already finished their dinner. _____
8. The train has already left. _____
9. We have learned many new words this week. _____
10. They have been married a long time. _____
11. She has been sick for several weeks. _____
12. They have been in Europe before. _____
13. He has lived in the United States a long time. _____
14. I have always liked to travel. _____
15. They have been friends since their high school days. _____
16. The mail has arrived. _____
17. The school bell has already rung. _____
18. He has always worked as a mechanic. _____
19. I have already had my lunch. _____
20. It has begun to rain. _____
21. All the girls have left. _____
22. He has always had rather strange ideas about money. _____

**SAY—TELL:** *Say* and *tell* have the same meaning in English but differ in the way they are used. When the sentence contains an indirect object (that is, when we mention the person to whom the words are spoken), we use *tell*. If there is no indirect object (that is, if we do not mention the person to whom the words are spoken), we use *say*. Examples:

He *said* that he was busy.
He *told me* that he was busy.
He *told John* that he was busy.

(We also use *tell* in the following constructions: *to tell the truth, to tell a lie, to tell a story, to tell time.*)

---

Write the correct form of *say* or *tell*, whichever is correct, in the blanks at the right.

1. The teacher ............ us (that)* he was too busy to see us. _____(told)_____
2. He ............ (that) he had too much work to do. _____
3. John ............ (that) English is difficult for him. _____
4. Can you ............ me where I can find Mr. Smith? _____
5. Alice ............ (that) she could not meet us after the lesson. _____
6. She ............ (that) she did not feel well. _____
7. George ............ me all about his trip to New York. _____
8. He ............ (that) he liked New York very much. _____
9. You can believe William because he always ............ the truth. _____
10. Henry ............ yesterday (that) he liked the new teacher very much. _____
11. He ............ (that) he understood every word she said. _____
12. He ............ both William and me (that) he planned to continue in her class. _____
13. I ............ Mr. Smith (that) I did not know how to typewrite. _____
14. He ............ (that) he could teach me easily. _____
15. It was John who ............ us (that) it was a good restaurant. _____
16. He ............ (that) he ate there every day. _____
17. I ............ them (that) I did not want to go to the movie. _____
18. William ............ (that) the book belonged to Mr. Smith. _____
19. I ............ him (that) I thought it belonged to Helen. _____
20. Who ............ you (that) Mr. Reese was an engineer? _____

* The word *that*, when used as a conjunction to introduce a subordinate clause as in these sentences, is often dropped in everyday speech. Thus we may say: "He said *that* he was busy." or "He said he was busy." Both forms are used and both are correct in English.

**REVIEW OF VERB FORMS:** In the blanks, write the *past tense* form and the *past participle* of each of the verbs below.

| | | Past | Past Part. | | | Past | Past Part. |
|---|---|---|---|---|---|---|---|
| 1. | see | (saw) | (seen) | 25. | eat | | |
| 2. | ask | (asked) | (asked) | 26. | fall | | |
| 3. | know | | | 27. | feel | | |
| 4. | get | | | 28. | study | | |
| 5. | arrive | | | 29. | live | | |
| 6. | have | | | 30. | fly | | |
| 7. | make | | | 31. | forget | | |
| 8. | find | | | 32. | give | | |
| 9. | grow | | | 33. | go | | |
| 10. | leave | | | 34. | hear | | |
| 11. | walk | | | 35. | be | | |
| 12. | show | | | 36. | end | | |
| 13. | say | | | 37. | mean | | |
| 14. | learn | | | 38. | meet | | |
| 15. | use | | | 39. | read | | |
| 16. | tell | | | 40. | ride | | |
| 17. | bring | | | 41. | ring | | |
| 18. | wait | | | 42. | run | | |
| 19. | begin | | | 43. | sell | | |
| 20. | break | | | 44. | talk | | |
| 21. | buy | | | 45. | shake | | |
| 22. | come | | | 46. | sleep | | |
| 23. | cost | | | 47. | speak | | |
| 24. | do | | | 48. | take | | |

**NEGATIVE FORM; REVIEW:** Change the sentences below to negative form. In the blanks to the right, write the necessary auxiliary verb followed by *not*. Also include the main verb, wherever possible. (See page 104 for a statement of the principles covering the formation of negatives in English.)

1. He speaks English well.        (does not speak) _____

2. They went to the movies with us last night. _____

3. They have delivered the mail. _____

4. It is beginning to rain. _____

5. He is a good student. _____

6. She left on the three o'clock train. _____

7. She will return on Wednesday. _____

8. He has many friends in this school. _____

9. He has gone out of town. _____

10. John was at the meeting last night. _____

11. They prepared their homework very well. _____

12. He comes to school by bus. _____

13. There is a magazine on the table. _____

14. Helen has studied English for a long time. _____

15. She began to study English in elementary school. _____

16. We waited a half hour for him. _____

17. He told us all about it. _____

18. I will be back in an hour. _____

19. I am going to the bookstore to buy some books. _____

20. He has worked in that office since 1950. _____

21. She can speak English perfectly. _____

22. You must tell him about it. _____

23. She writes many letters to her brother. _____

24. He put all his books on the teacher's desk. _____

122

**QUESTION FORM; REVIEW:** Change the sentences below to question form. In the blanks at the right, fill in the necessary auxiliary verb followed by the subject of the sentence. Also include the main verb, wherever possible. (See page 105 for a statement of the principles covering the formation of questions in English.)

---

1.  He comes to school by bus.                                          (Does he come)

2.  They live on Fifth Avenue.                                          ------------

3.  He went to Chicago last week.                                       ------------

4.  He will be there at least two weeks.                                ------------

5.  Helen wants to study American history next year.                   ------------

6.  She is an excellent student.                                        ------------

7.  She is going to study later in the United States.                  ------------

8.  Mr. Smith lent him the money.                                       ------------

9.  I saw him on the bus.                                               ------------

10. His wife was with him.                                             ------------

11. The bus was very crowded at the time.                             ------------

12. They have much work to do today.                                  ------------

13. He wrote me a letter about it.                                    ------------

14. He has studied English for a long time.                          ------------

15. He has on a white shirt and a blue tie.                          ------------

16. The wind is beginning to blow very hard.                         ------------

17. He can speak both French and Spanish.                            ------------

18. They go to the movies together every Saturday.                   ------------

19. They have seen all the latest pictures.                          ------------

20. He must come back later.                                         ------------

21. She threw all our compositions away.                            ------------

22. He was here on Wednesday.                                        ------------

23. They sit side by side at the lesson.                            ------------

24. She is feeling better today.                                    ------------

123

**POSITION OF INDIRECT OBJECT:** Certain common verbs such as *give,* *send, bring, write, tell* often have an indirect object, represented by a person's name or a pronoun, in addition to a direct object. If this indirect object follows the direct object, then the preposition *to* or *for* is used. If, however, the indirect object precedes the direct object, then no preposition is used.

He gave the money *to* me.
*or*  He gave *me* the money.

---

Re-state the following sentences, putting the indirect object before the direct object. In the blanks at the right, write the verb of each sentence followed by the indirect object.

1. He wrote a letter to her.                          (wrote her)
   ----------

2. She gave the money to her brother.
   ----------

3. He sent some postal cards to us.
   ----------

4. He brought some flowers to her.
   ----------

5. John wrote a letter to Mary.
   ----------

6. The teacher gave some homework to us.
   ----------

7. He told the story to us.
   ----------

8. We sent some flowers to Helen.
   ----------

9. He brought a box of candy to her.
   ----------

10. He gave a piece to each of us.
    ----------

11. I took the flowers to her.
    ----------

12. She lent some money to me.
    ----------

13. He sold the car to his friend.
    ----------

14. He bought a new suit for his son.
    ----------

15. Please bring the newspaper to me.
    ----------

16. I gave the tickets to Helen.
    ----------

17. She paid the money to me.
    ----------

18. I told the story to John.
    ----------

19. I sent money to her for her birthday.
    ----------

20. Don't show these pictures to Helen.
    ----------

21. He brought many presents to her from Europe.
    ----------

22. I will write a letter to you next week.
    ----------

**VOCABULARY REVIEW; OPPOSITES:** In the blanks to the right, write the opposites of the following words:

| | | | | | | |
|---|---|---|---|---|---|---|
| 1. | tall | (short) | 26. | clean | (dirty) |
| 2. | top | | 27. | few | |
| 3. | young | | 28. | sad | |
| 4. | beautiful | | 29. | absent | |
| 5. | often | | 30. | strong | |
| 6. | buy | | 31. | stop | |
| 7. | awake | | 32. | wrong | |
| 8. | borrow | | 33. | early | |
| 9. | loose | | 34. | poor | |
| 10. | high | | 35. | far | |
| 11. | laugh | | 36. | under | |
| 12. | sick | | 37. | easy | |
| 13. | inside | | 38. | better | |
| 14. | hard | | 39. | best | |
| 15. | dull | | 40. | dry | |
| 16. | push | | 41. | upstairs | |
| 17. | wide | | 42. | long | |
| 18. | empty | | 43. | first | |
| 19. | thick | | 44. | front | |
| 20. | behind | | 45. | same | |
| 21. | expensive | | 46. | north | |
| 22. | future | | 47. | east | |
| 23. | heavy | | 48. | warm | |
| 24. | sweet | | 49. | hot | |
| 25. | fat | | 50. | down | |

## WORDS USED AS NOUNS OR VERBS WITHOUT CHANGE IN FORM:

In most foreign languages a word may serve as only one part of speech; moreover, each part of speech has its special form or characteristics which serve to distinguish it from all other parts of speech. In English, however, there is a large group of words which may be used either as nouns or as verbs without any change in form. Observe how, in the following sentences, the word *work* is used as a verb in the first sentence and as a noun in the second sentence—without any change in form.

| | |
|---|---|
| (As a verb) | They *work* on the fourth floor. |
| (As a noun) | The *work* which they do is very interesting. |

---

The purpose of this exercise is to give you practice in recognizing the same word used sometimes as a noun and sometimes as a verb. In the blanks at the right, write NOUN if the italicized word of the sentence is used as a noun; write VERB if the italicized word is used as a verb.

1. We *look* up all the new words in our dictionaries.  (Verb)

   a) Everyone noticed the *look* of surprise on his face.  _____

2. We all enjoy the *study* of English.  _____

   a) They both *study* in the same class.  _____

3. Everyone heard the child's *cries*.  _____

   a) The baby *cries* all day long.  _____

4. John will *help* us when he comes.  _____

   a) We all need your *help* badly.  _____

5. Helen wore a very pretty *dress* to the party.  _____

   a) The baby is still too young to *dress* itself.  _____

6. Both buildings *face* the park.  _____

   a) The child has a beautiful *face*.  _____

7. After just a few *drinks* he became drunk.  _____

   a) John always *drinks* milk with his meals.  _____

8. We *plan* to go to Europe next summer.  _____

   a) The *plan* to attack England by air failed.  _____

9. All children *love* candy.  _____

   a) His *love* for her will never die.  _____

10. She has very good *taste* in clothes.  _____

   a) Most medicines *taste* very bitter.  _____

(Note: For additional practice using the same word as different parts of speech, make sentences with the following—use each word once as a noun and once as a verb: wish, finish, question, tie, talk, question, kiss, smile, shout, promise, play, surprise, start, walk, crowd, rest, fall, present, need, move, sound, notice, ride, turn, watch, etc.)

**CORRESPONDING NOUN AND VERB FORMS:** In the previous exercise, page 126, we saw how, in English, many words may serve as both nouns or verbs without any change in form. There is another large group of words, however, which cannot be used in this way; these words have one form as nouns and a different form as verbs. Observe these sample corresponding noun and verb combinations.

| *(Verb)* | *(Noun)* | *(Verb)* | *(Noun)* |
|---|---|---|---|
| to appear — appearance | | to describe — description | |
| to explain — explanation | | to lose — loss | |
| to arrive — arrival | | to decide — decision | |

---

In the blanks below, write the corresponding *noun form* of these verbs:

1. to explain      (explanation)
2. to collect      _____
3. to arrive      _____
4. to decide      _____
5. to prove      _____
6. to agree      _____
7. to believe      _____
8. to punish      _____
9. to remain      _____
10. to lose      _____

11. to observe      (observation)
12. to excite      _____
13. to die      _____
14. to choose      _____
15. to grow      _____
16. to marry      _____
17. to enter      _____
18. to begin      _____
19. to appear      _____
20. to repeat      _____

In the blanks below, write the corresponding *verb forms* of these nouns:

21. description      (to describe)
22. explanation      _____
23. satisfaction      _____
24. laughter      _____
25. growth      _____
26. existence      _____
27. proof      _____
28. agreement      _____
29. arrival      _____
30. location      _____

31. appearance      (to appear)
32. arrangement      _____
33. protection      _____
34. discovery      _____
35. explosion      _____
36. imagination      _____
37. loss      _____
38. failure      _____
39. entrance      _____
40. beginning      _____

**IDIOMATIC EXPRESSIONS:** Choose the correct form and write it in the blanks at the right.

1. The opposite of to *put on* is to (put away, take off, pick up, call on). _(take off)_ _____

2. The opposite of to *turn on* is to (turn down, turn off, put away, wait on). _____

3. To *get on* the bus is to (leave it, enter it, wait for it, signal to it). _____

4. I'd *rather study* means that I (like to study, study hard, prefer to study). _____

5. *Right away* means (much later, immediately, correct, wrong). _____

6. To *call up* someone is to (criticize him, meet him, like him, telephone him). _____

7. To *call on* someone is to (write to him, visit him, wait for him, telephone him). _____

8. To *get off* the bus is to (enter it, leave it, pay one's fare). _____

9. If I *take off* my coat, it means that I (put it on, remove it, hang it up, put it away). _____

10. The opposite of to *stand up* is to (leave, wait, sit down, arrive). _____

11. *At last* means (first, soon, finally, seldom). _____

12. If I am *tired out*, I am (rather tired, extremely tired, a little tired). _____

13. *Right here* means (near here, exactly here, over there). _____

14. To *look for* something is to (lose it, try to find it, need it, forget it). _____

15. If something is *all right*, this means that it is (out of order, satisfactory, ready, necessary). _____

16. *Little by little* means (soon, gradually, rapidly, never.) _____

17. To *find out* about something is to (remember it, get information about it, discuss it). _____

18. If someone says to you, "Look out!", this means (look out the window, wait, be careful). _____

19. To *talk over* something is to (discuss it, remember it, mention it, forget it). _____

20. If someone studies *by himself*, he studies (well, seldom, alone, seriously). _____

21. To *pick out* something means to (pick it up, throw it away, choose or select it, admire it). _____

22. To *make up one's mind* is to (study hard, remember something, decide something). _____

128

**PREPOSITIONS:** In the blanks to the right, fill in the correct prepositions needed to complete the meaning of each sentence.

1. He will be in Chicago ............ three days. ___(for)___

2. I am going to the cafeteria but I will be back ............ ten minutes. _____

3. I usually go to work ............ bus. _____

4. He always arrives in class ............ time. _____

5. I can finish this work ............ an hour. _____

6. He told me all ............ his trip to Europe. _____

7. I prefer to study ............ night. _____

8. There is almost no difference ............ these two books. _____

9. I am going to John's home ............ dinner. _____

10. He works ............ the sixth floor. _____

11. An airplane flew directly ............ our heads. _____

12. I paid two dollars ............ this book. _____

13. It is dark in this room. Please turn ............ the light. _____

14. Please explain ............ me what you mean. _____

15. I go ............ bed every night at eleven o'clock. _____

16. In the Civil War, the North fought ............ the South. _____

17. Helen is very much afraid ............ dogs. _____

18. Everybody laughed ............ him when he entered the room. _____

19. There is something wrong ............ this telephone. _____

20. He left the office ............ once after you called. _____

21. Please pick ............ those papers which are on the floor. _____

22. We waited and waited and ............ last he arrived. _____

23. I have lost my pen. Please help me to look ............ it. _____

24. She likes to look ............ herself in the mirror. _____

**VOCABULARY REVIEW; MISTAKES IN FACT:** In this exercise, correct the mistakes in fact by changing italicized word or words. Write the correct word or words in the blanks at the right.

1. There are *eight* days in a week.       (seven)

2. The largest city in the United States is *Chicago.*

3. Ten times five is *fifty-five.*

4. Fourteen minus four is *nine.*

5. There are *seventy* seconds in a minute.

6. The past tense of HIDE is *hidden.*

7. The past tense of BITE is *bitten.*

8. The plural form of SHEEP is *sheeps.*

9. The Pacific Ocean lies *east* of the United States.

10. The auxiliary verb which we use to form the present-perfect tense is *will.*

11. FIRST, SECOND, and THIRD are *cardinal* numbers.

12. There are *fourteen* inches in a foot.

13. We accent the word APARTMENT on the *third* syllable.

14. The word CAFETERIA has *four* syllables.

15. We pronounce the word ASKED as a word of *two* syllables.

16. We call all verbs which form their past tense by adding ED to the present tense *irregular* verbs.

17. The verb WALK is an *irregular* verb.

18. The verbs GO and SEE are *regular* verbs.

19. June is the *fifth* month of the year.

20. The sun always rises in the *west.*

21. The superlative form of the adjective COLD is *colder.*

22. Horses and dogs are *wild* animals.

23. We use the indefinite article AN before words which begin with a *consonant.*

24. The present century is the *nineteenth* century.

130

**VOCABULARY REVIEW:** Choose the correct word or words and write them in the blanks at the right.

1. The opposite of *big* is (old, new, little, large). _(little)_
2. The opposite of *wide* is (deep, high, narrow, big). _____
3. Which one of these verbs is in the past tense (run, jump, swam, kill)? _____
4. Which one of these verbs has the same form in the past tense as in the present tense (see, say, put, take, like)? _____
5. If I do something *by myself,* I do it (often, alone, quickly, slowly). _____
6. The adverb form of the adjective *good* is (better, well, best, worse). _____
7. Which one of these verbs is an "irregular" verb (walk, play, see, jump, talk)? _____
8. Which letter in the word *honest* is silent (not pronounced)? _____
9. Which letter in the word *answer* is silent (not pronounced)? _____
10. We pronounce the word *doubt* to rhyme with (but, caught, ought, out). _____
11. We pronounce the contraction *we're* to rhyme with (her, wear, where, fear, fire). _____
12. We pronounce the contraction *they're* to rhyme with (here, fair, four, fear). _____
13. A man *hears* with his (eyes, ears, nose, mouth). _____
14. Which one of these words is not spelled correctly: engineer, appearence, excellent, Wednesday, restaurant? _____
15. If it is very sharp, with which of these can you cut yourself easily (stove, cup, knife, saucer)? _____
16. We pronounce the word *cries* to rhyme with (sees, nice, size, raise). _____
17. The opposite of *married* is (alone, single, engaged, happy). _____
18. If I say that the lesson is *over,* this means that it (has just begun, has been long, has finished). _____
19. If I say that the time is *up,* this means that it (has just started, has ended, is about to end). _____
20. A closet is a place where we (hide, have lunch, meet our friends, hang our clothes). _____

**GENERAL REVIEW:** Choose the correct form and write it in the blanks at the right.

1. Listen! The telephone (rings, is ringing).      (is ringing)

2. John has worked in that office (since, for) many years.      _____

3. Helen (studied, has studied) English since January.      _____

4. He (said, told) that he was too busy to go with us.      _____

5. They have (much, many) friends in this town.      _____

6. He (lives, has lived) in New York for many years.      _____

7. She (does, makes) many mistakes in pronunciation.      _____

8. We (are, have been) friends for years.      _____

9. We (went, have gone) to the movies last night.      _____

10. I have never been in Washington (also, either).      _____

11. What time did you (left, leave) home this morning?      _____

12. It always (rains, is raining) very much during the month of April.      _____

13. I didn't see (anyone, someone) in the room.      _____

14. The weather today is warmer (than, as) it was yesterday.      _____

15. He gave (me, to me) all the money he had.      _____

16. There were (much, many) people present at the meeting.      _____

17. He (said, told) me that he could not come to the lesson.      _____

18. Hurry! William (waits, is waiting) for us.      _____

19. We (was, were) all late for the lesson.      _____

20. He wants (us to wait, that we wait) for him.      _____

21. We (are going, go) to school every day together.      _____

22. They (have, are having) their lunch now.      _____

23. The dog chases (it's, its) own tail.      _____

24. The teacher explained (us, to us) the meaning of each word.      _____

132

# PRINCIPAL PARTS OF IRREGULAR VERBS

| Present | Past | Perfect | Present | Past | Perfect |
|---------|------|---------|---------|------|---------|
| be | was | been | lose | lost | lost |
| become | became | become | make | made | made |
| begin | began | begun | mean | meant | meant |
| blow | blew | blown | meet | met | met |
| break | broke | broken | pay | paid | paid |
| bring | brought | brought | put | put | put |
| buy | bought | bought | read | read | read |
| catch | caught | caught | ride | rode | ridden |
| come | came | come | ring | rang | rung |
| cost | cost | cost | run | ran | run |
| cut | cut | cut | say | said | said |
| do | did | done | see | saw | seen |
| drink | drank | drunk | sell | sold | sold |
| drive | drove | driven | send | sent | sent |
| eat | ate | eaten | shake | shook | shaken |
| fall | fell | fallen | shoot | shot | shot |
| feel | felt | felt | shut | shut | shut |
| fight | fought | fought | sing | sang | sung |
| find | found | found | sit | sat | sat |
| fly | flew | flown | sleep | slept | slept |
| forget | forgot | forgotten | speak | spoke | spoken |
| get | got | gotten | spend | spent | spent |
| give | gave | given | stand | stood | stood |
| go | went | gone | steal | stole | stolen |
| grow | grew | grown | sweep | swept | swept |
| have | had | had | take | took | taken |
| hear | heard | heard | teach | taught | taught |
| hit | hit | hit | tell | told | told |
| hold | held | held | think | thought | thought |
| hurt | hurt | hurt | throw | threw | thrown |
| keep | kept | kept | understand | understood | understood |
| know | knew | known | wear | wore | worn |
| leave | left | left | win | won | won |
| lend | lent | lent | write | wrote | written |

# SAMPLE CONJUGATIONS

Verb: *To be*

### Present Tense

| | |
|---|---|
| I am | we are |
| you are | you are |
| he, she, it is | they are |

### Future Tense

| | |
|---|---|
| I shall be | we shall be |
| you will be | you will be |
| he will be | they will be |

### Past Tense

| | |
|---|---|
| I was | we were |
| you were | you were |
| he was | they were |

### Present Perfect Tense

| | |
|---|---|
| I have been | we have been |
| you have been | you have been |
| he has been | they have been |

Verb: *To work* (Simple form)

### Present Tense

| | |
|---|---|
| I work | we work |
| you work | you work |
| he, she, it works | they work |

### Future Tense

| | |
|---|---|
| I shall work | we shall work |
| you will work | you will work |
| he will work | they will work |

### Past Tense

| | |
|---|---|
| I worked | we worked |
| you worked | you worked |
| he worked | they worked |

### Present Perfect Tense

| | |
|---|---|
| I have worked | we have worked |
| you have worked | you have worked |
| he has worked | they have worked |

Verb: *To work* (Continuous form)

### Present Tense

| | |
|---|---|
| I am working | we are working |
| you are working | you are working |
| he, she, it is working | they are working |